THE NOBI

Nihil Obstat:
Rev. William Wilson
Censor deputatis

Imprimatur:
+ Rt Rev. Philip A. Egan BA, STL, PhD
Bishop of Portsmouth
15 October 2019

The Nihil Obstat and Imprimatur are official declarations that a book or pamphlet is free of doctrinal or moral error. No implication is contained therein that those who have granted the Nihil Obstat and Imprimatur agree with the contents, opinions or statements expressed.

THE NOBLE MARTYR

A Spiritual Biography of St Philip Howard

DUDLEY PLUNKETT

GRACEWING

First published in England in 2019
by
Gracewing
2 Southern Avenue
Leominster
Herefordshire HR6 0QF
United Kingdom
www.gracewing.co.uk

The publishers have no responsibility for the
persistence or accuracy of URLs for websites referred
to in this publication, and do not guarantee that any
content on such websites is, or will remain, accurate
or appropriate.

ISBN 978 085244 959 2

Typeset by Word and Page, Chester, UK
Cover design by Bernardita Peña Hurtado

CONTENTS

Front cover illustration
St Philip's statue in Arundel Cathedral,
carved (*c.* 1970) by Ivor Hursey in limewood
Photo: Justine Claire

FOREWORD

It was pacing up and down the Long Gallery here at Arundel Castle that four hundred years ago my ancestor Philip Howard, Earl of Arundel, made his fateful decision to become reconciled to the Catholic faith. It is extraordinary to be the direct descendant of a canonised saint, a man who was attainted and sentenced to death by Queen Elizabeth at the age of 27 (although Queen Elizabeth could never bring herself to carry his execution out). However, he remained imprisoned in the Tower until his death from poisoning eleven years later at the age of 38.

It was another of my ancestors, the 14th Duke, who was responsible, in 1857, for editing a precious manuscript by an unknown Jesuit priest which has preserved for posterity almost all we know about the life of St Philip. Dudley Plunkett's work is therefore to be welcomed for looking again at the saint's life by going back to his reading and writing during the time he spent in the Tower of London. From these sources he deduces valuable information and insights that attest to the character and sanctity of a man who accepted being deprived of his privileged life as the premier earl of the kingdom, and even of his wife and children, out of commitment to his faith.

I especially welcome a book about St Philip that combines scholarly research with spiritual sensitivity and thus offers a reminder of the courage and fidelity of our ancestors with more than a historian's interest. For example, Dr Plunkett's study places great emphasis upon St Philip's devotion to the Blessed Virgin. It was in fact another member of my family, Thomas, younger son of Richard Fitzalan, the 10th Earl of Arundel, who, as Archbishop of Canterbury, wrote of the Virgin to his suffragan bishops in 1399:

> The contemplation of the great mystery of the Incarnation has drawn all Christian nations to venerate her from whom came the first beginnings of our redemption. But

we English, being the servants of her special inheritance
and her own dowry, as we are commonly called, ought
to surpass others in the fervour of our praises and
devotions.

This tradition so dear to the heart of medieval English people,
rejected by the Reformers but firmly retained by recusant
Catholics, had an important influence on the spiritual life of
St Philip. The statue from his shrine illustrated on the cover
of the book makes the point by showing a rosary in his hand.
Whether or not he was aware of what a distinguished member
of his family had written two hundred years earlier, Philip
would have been among those who thought of England as
Mary's Dowry, and he must have rejoiced in heaven when it
was announced that the bishops of this country planned to
rededicate England to Mary in 2020.

The hope of today's world must lie, as Dr Plunkett sees it in
concluding his book, in a Church rebuilt in the lives of a new
generation of saints, inspired by the example of the martyrs of
these lands and helped by the powerful means of their prayers.
Such must have been the belief of St Philip and of those who
were persecuted for their faith in his time, and no doubt they
are rejoicing at any signs that their suffering was not in vain.

Edward Fitzalan-Howard, 18th Duke of Norfolk

Acknowledgements

I gratefully acknowledge the support and contributions made by several people: the Sisters of Tyburn Convent, for their inspiration and prayers; the Rt Rev. Dom Geoffrey Scott OSB, Abbot and Librarian of Douai Abbey, for getting me started on the trail of St Philip Howard; the Librarian of the Jesuits in Britain Archive; the Very Rev. Canon Tim Madeley, Dean of Arundel Cathedral, and Very Rev Canon Jonathan Martin VG, Diocese of Arundel and Brighton, for their encouragement and helpfulness; the Rev. Martin Plunkett, my son, and my wife, Francine, for many useful conversations and insights; the Duke of Norfolk, for his kindness in contributing a Foreword to the book; the Staff of Gracewing, for their advice and patience.

INTRODUCTION

P HILIP HOWARD, EARL OF ARUNDEL (1557–95), son of the 4th Duke of Norfolk, reached adulthood forty years after the execution of Thomas More and John Fisher when the Elizabethan Reformation was well under way. No less than 819 monastic communities had been dissolved by Henry VIII; the Mass and even the Rosary had been banned under Elizabethan legislation; the iconoclasts had ransacked shrines and churches; the law had proscribed the practice of the Catholic faith; the new religion of the Church of England had repudiated many of the principal teachings of the Catholic Church including the doctrine of transubstantiation; a succession of laws held anyone identified as a Catholic priest guilty of treason and liable to fines, imprisonment, torture and even execution; and 183 English Catholics were put to death between 1577 and 1603.

In many ways Philip's fate can be compared to that of his great spiritual precursor, Thomas More. Both were highly placed courtiers of the reigning monarch. Both were conscientious objectors to the Act of Supremacy which affirmed the monarch's claim to be supreme head of the Church in England. Both were imprisoned in the Tower of London and sentenced to death. Both showed a forgiving spirit and died reconciled in their hearts to those who had condemned them. Unlike Thomas, Philip did not hold any public office, but he had the standing of the country's premier earl, and his repudiation of the newly established Church was potentially very injurious to Queen Elizabeth's claims. However, he was guilty of nothing other than obeying his conscience and in this offers a timeless inspiration similar to that of St Thomas More.

In 1857, three hundred years after Philip's birth, his descendant, Henry Granville Fitzalan-Howard, 14th Duke of Norfolk, published a 27,000-word manuscript in his possession, the first part of which is entitled 'The Life and Death of the Renowned

Confessor Philip Howard, Earl of Arundel'.[1] This is an arresting title for its ascription 'renowned confessor'. Indeed, St Philip was a great confessor of the Catholic faith, and for this he was canonised, but it is undoubtedly true that his renown is less than he deserves. He stands to be recognised as a significant saint who attracted the respect of many contemporaries, Protestants as well as Catholics, for his personal virtue and valour, despite being a victim of prejudice, injustice and cruelty.

The main source for the details of St Philip's life has been the near-contemporary manuscript (Arundel manuscript – AM). Although there is no author cited in the manuscript, and the Duke does not suggest any name, the document itself states that its author is a Jesuit priest (AM, p. 222) who resided as chaplain with Countess Anne Howard, Philip's wife, for the last fourteen years of her life, that is 1616–30 (AM, pp. 202 and 209). Although there are two parts to the manuscript, the separate biographies of Philip and of his wife, both are clearly from the same author. This is apparent from the style of writing, their similar structure, the constant references to familiarity with the life and religious devotions of Countess Anne, the access to letters between the spouses as well as to letters between St Robert Southwell SJ, who had also resided with Anne Howard, and St Philip, and the known link between Anne and the Jesuit Order, whose novitiate in Ghent she supported financially (AM, p. 219).

We also have the text of the letter Philip wrote to the Queen before his attempted departure from England and other letters written from the Tower of London to major figures concerning his situation, including a letter of protestation of his innocence of any crime of treason. Many of the documents cited by the author of the Arundel manuscript have been located elsewhere by Pollen and MacMahon.[2] This allows us to verify that he cites accurately, which enables us to trust him even when his sources are not available to us, though allowing for a certain

1   H. G. Fitzalan-Howard, Duke of Norfolk (ed.), *The Lives of Philip Howard, Earl of Arundel, and of Anne Dacres, his Wife*, 1857.
2   J. H. Pollen and W. MacMahon, *Unpublished Documents Relating to the English Martyrs* (London: Catholic Record Society, 1908–19).

amount of hagiographical bias on the part of someone who evidently had a great regard for the Howard family. Given the paucity of sources from which to sketch out St Philip's life, there is every justification for a fuller biography than the Arundel manuscript or the other brief accounts that have since been published of such an outstanding representative of the recusant laity in some of the harshest years of the Elizabethan persecution of Catholics.

It was following a visit to the Martyrs' Chapel at the Tyburn Convent that the possibility of a spiritual biography of one of the Forty Martyrs of England and Wales occurred to me, and in the succeeding days the idea of this book began to form in my mind. Some weeks later, I visited the Arundel shrine of St Philip, co-patron of the diocese of Arundel and Brighton, and resolved to pursue the work, taking St Philip as a major figure among the forty martyrs and a representative of all whose lives were forfeit in the Elizabethan persecutions. I am not intending the kind of hagiography that risks exaggerating the subject's virtues and holiness, and which has acquired a bad name in a secular culture that easily banishes saints from its consciousness. True hagiography, however, does not exaggerate or falsify, but instead appreciates, values, confirms and thanks God and the Church for exposing to us the merits and wisdom of the saints and for the knowledge that they are with God and can help and guide those who appeal to their aid. They are spiritual giants whom we can spur to action through our prayers. They can prompt us to seek God's solution to our woes and the path of our own salvation.

I hope that this work will speak to those who might be interested not only in the historical person that was Philip Howard, Earl of Arundel, but also in how the lives of saints like Philip have relevance for our society and culture today. As one of the forty canonised martyrs of England and Wales, St Philip surely retains a significant role as an intercessor and inspiration for Catholic life. These martyrs and many other saints are waiting for a new time for the Faith as the fruit of their sacrifice allied to that of their Lord. Notably, in a famous sermon, St John Henry Newman appeals to God to answer the prayers of the martyrs on account of their generous sufferings:

Can we religiously suppose that the blood of our martyrs, three centuries ago and since, shall never receive its recompense?. . . The long imprisonment, the fetid dungeon, the weary suspense, the tyrannous trial, the barbarous sentence, the savage execution, the rack, the gibbet, the knife, the cauldron, the numberless tortures of those holy victims. O my God, are they to have no reward? Are thy martyrs to cry from under thine altar for their loving vengeance on this guilty people, and to cry in vain? Shall they lose life, and not gain a better life for the children of those who persecuted them?[3]

Martyrs are those who witness not only with their lives but also with their deaths. The life-blood of martyrs is claimed to be the seed of the Church, of its holiness and renewal. So the Church of today can benefit by having recourse to the intercession and graces merited by the martyrs of the Penal Times who so willingly went to the scaffold. St Philip was anxious to go to execution on Tower Hill rather than to die in his bed, as in fact happened, but he is regarded as a witness unto death. These people died for the Faith, and so we can be certain that they are praying for its survival in our times.

The documentation regarding St Philip that is available to us, with the exception of the Arundel manuscript, is largely concerned with his two trials, and not his years as a prisoner in the Tower of London. Unlike some of the others among the forty martyrs, whose religious colleagues made a record of their lives, Philip did not belong to a religious order, and consequently we have much less documentary information about him.[4] The result is that we are obliged to rely upon the Arundel manuscript for any direct evidence as to his spiritual life and development. As regards indirect evidence, we look for signs and guideposts for understanding Philip's interior life by examining the influences to which he was exposed at

---

[3] St John Henry Newman, *Second Spring* (sermon) (http://www. newmanreader.org).

[4] Contrast this with the highly detailed account of the activities of his Jesuit priest antecedents in England in the same period in P. Caraman, *Henry Garnet 1555–1605 and the Gunpowder Plot* (London: Longman, Green & Co., 1964).

the time of his conversion, and subsequently. These mainly consist in what he read or wrote, especially during his years of imprisonment. No one apart from the author of the Arundel manuscript appears to have made a substantial effort to capture his spirit, and I see the possibility that there is a deeper story that can be retrieved from a close study of the principal works that he studied, translated and authored around the time of his reconciliation to the Catholic Church and during his time in the Tower.

By identifying some of the main spiritual themes that emerge from these texts we can see what ideas and insights preoccupied Philip and which help to explain his extraordinary faith and zeal, which never flagged despite all the injustice and ill-treatment that he was made to suffer for the last decade of his life. Through what may be termed a spiritual biography, I hope to illuminate his interior life in a way that has not been attempted previously, and then to see how this Elizabethan layman can be an exemplar of Christian life for a different age. I also seek to place our contemporary society under the spiritual spotlight of the martyr-saint so as to find his inspiration for addressing many of the issues that wrack a society singularly bereft of the light of divine Truth.

Finally, I take a wider view, considering how the Elizabethan martyrs have been neglected and need to be reclaimed if we are to do them justice for their great sufferings and holiness by invoking their merits and prayers for the renewal of faith in England, and indeed in all Western societies today where the Faith has become so diminished. If they were able to resist to the death the proscriptions and persecution of their time, and so contribute to the survival of the Catholic faith over the ensuing centuries, we need to recover their spirit and their strength to ensure the flourishing of that faith so essential to humanity in a secular age.

I begin, however, by outlining St Philip's life, the details of which can be found, with varying degrees of thoroughness, in several other sources up until the time of his trial for treason. This biographical account is needed as the basis for interpreting his prison experience, which is the part of his life on which I am especially concentrating. I want to reflect on the available evidence as to the graces he received to persevere to the end of his harrowing confinement in the Tower of London, and to understand in what his sanctity and martyr status consisted.

It might be thought that the spirituality of a sixteenth-century saint, with its emphasis on pious devotions, fasts, self-denial and self-humiliating prayers, is not relevant for today's Christians, but this is an injudicious viewpoint to take. The saints throughout the ages have followed the Gospel and the teachings of the New Testament in seeing the contrast between the majesty of God and the apparent worthlessness or nothingness of the individual person. This is a spirituality that has been disregarded in recent decades but surely not replaced by the often self-preoccupied spiritualities proposed by many contemporary writers.

The Life of Philip Howard in Outline

AS A CHILD, A STUDENT AND A COURTIER

1557   Philip Howard, 19th Earl of Arundel, was born the only child of Thomas, Duke of Norfolk and Lady Mary Fitzalan, daughter of Henry, 18th Earl of Arundel. His mother died within a month of giving birth. The Duke later had two sons (Thomas and William) and a daughter (Margaret) by his second wife who also predeceased him. His third wife was Lady Dacre, who already had one son, Francis, who died in an accident, and three daughters. Philip was baptised a Catholic in the Queen's Chapel in Whitehall, in the presence of Queen Mary and the King Consort, King Philip of Spain, who was his godfather, but he was brought up as a Protestant following the death of Queen Mary in 1558 and the accession of Elizabeth to the throne. His father had come under the influence of John Foxe, the Protestant martyrologist, who was his tutor at his aunt the Duchess of Richmond's house, his mother having died giving birth to him.

Gregory Martin, who was a friend of Edmund Campion, became Philip's tutor, and no doubt influenced him in his attitude to the Catholic Church, even though Martin did not become a Catholic until he left the Duke of Norfolk's service.

1569   Philip is married to Anne Dacre, his step-sister, mainly in order to be able to inherit from his step-mother's estate.

1571   The marriage is repeated to ensure its validity, as Philip was not of the full age of consent in 1569.

1572 The execution of Philip's father, the Duke of Norfolk, after he proposed marriage to Mary Queen of Scots, amid suspicion that he was plotting treason.

1572 Philip studies at St John's College, Cambridge, for two years but does not complete his degree.

1575–80 Philip attends the court of Queen Elizabeth, to whom he was related, and becomes a royal favourite. He neglected his wife and rarely saw her during this time.

The writer of the Arundel manuscript passes over in silence some misdemeanours of which the future saint was guilty at Cambridge and at the Court, referring to them as 'inconveniences' and at another point to the 'exceeding liberty wherein he lived while he was a Protestant' (AM, p. 112), but it is important to cite them as they undoubtedly contributed to the strength of his later conversion or reconciliation to the Catholic faith. Philip wasted much of his money on sport and feasting, and spent huge sums entertaining the Queen at his homes in Norwich and in London.

HIS CONVERSION
AND RECONCILIATION WITH HIS WIFE

1580 Philip Howard succeeds to his mother's inheritance upon the death of his grandfather, thus becoming Earl of Arundel.

1581 Philip was reportedly present at the disputation held in the Tower of London, between Fathers Edmund Campion and Ralph Sherwin and a group of Protestant theologians.

1582 Margaret, Philip's half-sister, who had married Robert Sackville, is reconciled to the Church. She was close friends with Anne Howard, Philip's wife.

1584 Philip has a moment of grace at Arundel Castle when, walking in a gallery which is now the library, he decided that he believed in the truth of the Catholic faith, and shortly thereafter he was reconciled to the Church with his brother William by Fr William Weston, a missionary priest. After his reconciliation he arranged to have a priest at his London home in order to be able to attend daily Mass.

HIS ARREST AND TRIAL

1584 Philip attends the sessions of Parliament from 26 November 1584 to 29 March 1585 (AM, p. 98) and takes his turn in the court ceremonies (AM, p. 105).

1585 Fearing persecution, because adhering to the Catholic faith was illegal and considered treasonous, and feeling he was coming under suspicion, he attempts to leave the country after composing a long letter of explanation to the Queen (AM, pp. 31–51). This he left with his sister, Margaret Sackville, to be transmitted to Elizabeth after he had departed (AM, p.30). Such was the vigilance exercised over him that his letter was discovered before it had even been delivered. His intended flight from the country was made known through betrayal by a servant. He was arrested while setting sail from Littlehampton and imprisoned in the Tower of London on 25 April 1585.

After his arrest he was examined on various occasions by representatives of the Queen and later formally charged in the Star Chamber on 17 May 1586 with a long list of offences: harbouring of priests; being reconciled to Rome; attempting to leave the realm without licence from the Queen; being in communication with Dr Allen, the exiled English cardinal; and soliciting a bull of excommunication against the Queen. In the examinations he acknowledged that he was a Catholic, that he had already set forth his reasons for leaving the kingdom in his letter to the Queen which had been made public, that there was nothing treasonous in his letter to Dr Allen, and that no such bull of excommunication had been formulated. In short, he maintained strongly that he was innocent of all charges except that of being a Catholic. In the end the charge of high treason was not sustained, despite an attempt to introduce a fake letter said to be from him and referring to treasonous plans, but he was sentenced to a fine of £10,000 and imprisonment at the Queen's pleasure in the Tower of London, where he remained until his death nearly eleven years later. His brother William and his sister Margaret both suffered imprisonment for being reconciled to the Catholic Church.

1586   Fr Robert Southwell, a Jesuit missionary priest, arrives in England and is lodged as chaplain to Countess Anne Howard at Arundel House in The Strand and commences a series of letters to Philip.

The Earl is confined in the Beauchamp Tower, where he left a famous inscription still visible today on the wall of his cell. *Quanto plus afflictiones pro Christo in hoc saeculo, tanto plus gloriae cum Christo in futuro. Arundell June 22 1587* (The more afflictions for Christ in this world, the more glory with Christ in the next).

1588   For a time Philip is allowed greater liberty in the Tower and is even able to attend Masses said by a fellow inmate, Fr William Bennet. However, Fr Bennet later betrayed him at his trial by alleging that he had asked for a Mass to be said for the Catholic cause at the time of the Spanish Armada.

1589   Following the rout of the Armada, officials of the Council were again dispatched to question Philip about the Mass said in the Tower. He denied that it had been for the success of the Armada and maintained that it had simply been for the good estate of Catholics and their preparation for whatever fate might await them from official or popular reactions at the landing of the Spaniards.

Philip was arraigned a second time, on this occasion before the King's Bench in Westminster Hall on 14 April 1589, for having favoured the excommunication of the Queen and for having prayed for the invaders. The Earl claimed that his prayers had not been for any political cause. He was found guilty and condemned to death for treason, a sentence which was not carried out since the Queen never signed the death warrant, possibly because of the public outcry against the guilty verdict.

The conduct of the trial was described by Pollen and Mac-Mahon as follows:

> Though Philip Howard was still quite a young man, who had passed by far the greater part of his life under the tutelage or the wardship of Tudor teachers or jailors, his trial was a cause celebre. The Earl had become a

Catholic, and he was now the highest representative of the old church in England. The lawyers, whom the Tudors knew so well how to use, were now under Elizabeth's own eye to do their best to annihilate him in the face of the world. He had committed no offence whatever against the Queen or against the realm. The laws against liberty of conscience he had indeed transgressed, but the Government would not attain its object if it rested solely or too patently on that point. They must create the impression that the innocent man, sealed up in his cell, is really the active, ubiquitous, unscrupulous plotter: hand and glove with assassins, the potent ally of hostile invaders, moving the Pope to action by his letters, ambitioning the crown of England. This can only be done by great liberty of invective, by throwing mud immeasurable, by dragging in every charge which the anti-Catholic fanatics had accepted. We must be prepared for, and we find, endless accusations, innumerable innuendoes, numberless false issues, irrelevant and elusive evidence, few witnesses alleging no valid evidence. The accused, neither warned nor prepared, is allowed no adequate opportunity for defence. The verdict, as always in these trials for treason, is unanimous for the Crown.[1]

A matter neglected in the biographies of St Philip, but which was noted by Robinson in his chapter on St Philip in his work on the dukes of Norfolk,[2] concerns the Earl of Derby, who presided over his King's Bench trial for high treason and later confessed that he had been unconvinced by the evidence. Robinson references Goodman, who provides a fuller account of the Earl of Derby's misgivings:

> At first his offence was made but a matter of misdemeanour, and he was fined and censured in the Star Chamber very deeply; afterwards it seemed some letter was produced, and thereby he was questioned upon point of high treason; the Earl of Derby was then

[1] Pollen and MacMahon, *Unpublished Documents*, p. 232.
[2] J. M. Robinson, *The Dukes of Norfolk* (Chichester: Phillimore, 1995), p. 76.

appointed high steward, and before him Arundel was arraigned and found guilty. A little after, the Earl of Derby returned home to his own house, Latham, in Lancashire, and while he was on his journey he found himself much troubled with sorrow and melancholy; and doubting his own life, but especially desiring to discharge his own conscience, he caused all his servants to be called up into his chamber, and there did acquaint them thus much, that he had been more beholden to Queen Elizabeth than ever any of his predecessors had been to any prince; that she had conferred many favours upon him, that she had made him her ambassador in a business of great trust, and had ever used him most graciously; but this one thing did grieve him more than all the favours that he had received from her, that she had made him her high steward to condemn the Earl of Arundel, who was condemned upon a letter which, as he thought, was not sufficiently proved, but may be very well counterfeited, 'and this lies heavy upon my conscience'.[3]

Although subject to severe examination and threats, Fr Bennet deserves the chief blame for Philip's guilty verdict. He was a true-life Vicar of Bray figure who had not only conformed to the Church of England before being reconciled to the Catholic Church, but gave written evidence against Philip on 15 October 1588, later confessed his treachery and lies in letters to Philip and to his wife, and then again testified against the Earl at his King's Bench trial. What does all this say about the state of justice in the realm? A person appointed by the Queen to oversee the trial of a major figure for the crime of high treason expresses his doubt about the evidence, but after the trial, when he had allowed the accused to be condemned to death. Justice was forgotten by a new Pontius Pilate-like crowd-pleaser. Such was the regime that Philip had to contend with. He had no hope of proving his innocence.

---

[3]   G. Goodman, *The Court of King James the First* (Boston: Adamant Media Corp., 2002), vol. 1, pp. 139–44.

HIS IMPRISONMENT

Philip's life as a courtier and his life in prison were in total contrast. There was a complete change in his material circumstances through the filth and discomfort of his cell and the treatment meted out to him such that he reproached his jailer, the superintendent of the Tower, as he lay dying. Although there is little written about his inner life, it is important to consider what we do know, based on some few biographical details. He was kept virtually in solitary confinement for the first 13 months of his imprisonment and suffered much mistreatment especially by many former friends and associates who slandered him and sought to turn the Queen further against him.

Philip writes a letter pleading his innocence of the crimes of which he was accused, in case he was not allowed to speak at his execution (AM, pp. 99–102).

1591 The death of Margaret Sackville, half-sister to Philip.

1592 Southwell is betrayed, arrested and imprisoned in the Tower and Newgate.

1595 Fr Robert Southwell is executed on 2 February, aged 33.

HIS DEATH

1595 Philip petitions the Queen to be allowed to see his wife and the son he had never seen. The Queen sent back a verbal message that he could do so, and have his title restored, if he would but attend a Protestant service, but he declines the offer under these conditions.

In August, Philip is taken violently ill while eating, and this led to dysentery from which he did not recover for the remaining weeks of his life. There was a suspicion of poisoning which could not be confirmed, but in a letter to his wife some time before this he refers to the possibility that some harm is intended to him, so he may have had warning of such a danger. At all events, when Countess Anne later transferred his body from the Tower chapel to Arundel Castle, she included in the inscription on the iron coffin she had prepared the words *non absque veneni suspitione in Domino obdormivit* (he died in the Lord, not without suspicion of poisoning).

Philip dies on 19 October 1595, aged 38.

The Influence of Philip's Reading on his Interior Life

T HERE IS VERY LITTLE DIRECT EVIDENCE about Philip's interior life and yet, based on what is known, the Catholic Church beatified him in 1930 and then canonised him a saint and a martyr in 1970. When we consider indirect evidence, we are reliant principally on the Arundel manuscript which was compiled some thirty years after his death by the anonymous Jesuit priest who resided in the home of the Countess of Arundel. As her chaplain, he had access to correspondence between Philip and his wife and to letters exchanged between Philip and Fr Robert Southwell, who served as chaplain to Countess Anne until he was arrested in 1592. Further and even more indirect testimony to Philip's sanctity can be sought in his reading and translation work during his time in the Tower.

In this chapter, reference will be made to works that we know or have good reasons for assuming that Philip studied, and which very likely contributed to his spiritual formation. He was a serious reader, as the Arundel manuscript reports. From this and other sources we can identify several significant works to which he had access, among the probably very many other works that he read before his trial or that reached him in the Tower. In the following chapter the focus is upon writings that Philip left, including several letters, translation work and a number of poems.

When deciding how to study what Philip read and wrote in an attempt to gauge the impact on his interior life, it seemed logical to review the material in its chronological order in so far as this can be established, as it is reasonable to assume that there was a progression in the spiritual order that deepened his inner life to the culminating point of his death. We can hope to discover what were the themes he most likely dwelt on in his reading and writing. How did this reading change him? What do his reading and his writing reveal to us about the development of his faith and spiritual life?

THE INFLUENCE OF A FELLOW MARTYR

St Edmund Campion was a contemporary of Philip's who, like him, had had a gilded youth. He was not of noble stock but had made a brilliant success of his Oxford student career and, when ordained deacon in the Church of England in 1569, was destined for high rank in the Anglican Church until he suddenly converted to Catholicism and went overseas to join the Jesuit Order. When he returned as a priest on the English mission he wrote two works questioning the legitimacy of the new Church that earned him public notoriety. These were his challenge to the Privy Council, which became known as Campion's *Brag*, and the *Decem Rationes*, or ten reasons that he addressed to 'the learned members of the Universities of Oxford and Cambridge' to explain his cause:

> to make good to you the account of my conduct; to show you the chief heads and point my finger to the sources from whence I derive this confidence; to exhort you also, as it is your concern above others, to give to this business that attention which Christ, the Church, the Common Weal, and your own salvation demand of you. (*Decem Rationes*, 'Preface')

In his writings Campion had asked for a public disputation with representatives of the Church of England. However, it was only after his arrest, imprisonment and torture that this request was granted. It eventually took place in four sessions at the Tower of London in August and September of 1581. By this time Campion had been severely racked and he was denied the opportunity to prepare for the debate and had to remain standing for hours without any notes. None the less he made a sterling defence of his position and, according to the Arundel manuscript, Philip was deeply impressed by his evident holiness. His trial, at which Philip was present, ensued in Westminster Hall on 20 November 1581 when the Privy Council called on false testimony to back the charges of treason. Campion was found guilty and sentenced to be hanged, drawn and quartered.

It is worth considering the striking words spoken by Campion at his trial, which Philip would have heard:

> It was not our death that ever we feared. But we knew that we were not lords of our own lives, and therefore for want of answer would not be guilty of our own deaths. The only thing that we have now to say is that if our religion does make us traitors we are worthy to be condemned; but otherwise we are and have been as true subjects as ever the Queen had. In condemning us you condemn all your own ancestors, all the ancient priests, Bishops and Kings: all that was once the glory of England, the Island of Saints, and the most devoted child of the See of Peter.[1]

We can only surmise how Philip was led to be reconciled to the Catholic Church after attending Edmund Campion's disputation and trial. The impact of the events was unexpectedly sudden, but he needed time to absorb their significance, to take up the text of Campion's *Brag* and the *Decem Rationes* at leisure, to reflect upon them, and see with what justice, probity and valour Campion makes his defence as a loyal subject of the Queen yet a member of the Catholic faith and a Jesuit priest. Since he had three years between attending the disputation and trial and his own reconciliation with the Church, it would have been natural for him to follow up the sources of the convincing case that the future martyr had made in any way he could.

At all events, after witnessing Campion's trial, Philip left the court, renounced his previous, frivolous life and sought reconciliation with his wife who had recently returned to the

---

[1]   https://catholicinsight.com/the-diamond-of-england-the-mission-and-martyrdom-of-st-edmund-campion.

Catholic faith of her childhood. They then had two children, Elizabeth and Thomas, the son Philip was never to see. For her returning to the Catholic Church, the Queen ordered Anne to be a prisoner in the house of Sir Thomas Shirley in Sussex. Anne was pregnant and gave birth to a daughter whom Philip arranged to have baptised a Protestant, much against Anne's will, and named Elizabeth. But this effort at reconciliation with the Queen failed, and it was the last time that Philip made any kind of religious compromise.

Reading the *Brag*, Philip would have associated himself with its confession of Catholicism, for by his subsequent unrepentant attitude and his status as a known recusant he affirmed his belonging to the old Catholic faith. In effect he followed the same path of renunciation as Edmund Campion, who, 'resigned all my interest or possibilitie of wealth, honour, pleasure, and other worldlie felicitie' (*Brag*, 1). Further, Philip clearly renounced any political ambitions, as did Edmund: 'I never had mind ... to deal in any respect with matter of State or Policy of this realm, as things which appertain not to my vocation' (*Brag*, 4). He had witnessed personally to the truth of Edmund's challenge:

> I know perfectly that no one Protestant, nor all the Protestants living, nor any sect of our adversaries (howsoever they face men down in pulpits and overrule us in their kingdom of grammarians and unlearned ears) can maintain their doctrine in disputation. (*Brag*, 6)

Edmund hoped that the Queen might lessen her pursuit of Catholics: 'that possibly her zeal of truth and love of her people shall incline her noble Grace to disfavour some proceedings hurtful to the Realm, and procure towards us oppressed more equitie' (*Brag*, 7). Finally, he affirms the absolute determination of faithful Catholics, student priests and members of the Jesuit Order, to seek to win the souls of those in error, to the point of death:

> Many innocent hands are lifted up to Heaven for you daily by those English students, whose posteritie shall never die, which beyond seas, gathering virtue and sufficient knowledge for the purpose, are determined

never to give you over, but either to win you Heaven,
or to die upon your pikes. *(Brag, 8)*

Philip would adopt these same views, as his two major letters,
to the Queen and to the public whom he expected to attend
his execution, give clear testimony.

As regards the *Decem Rationes*, it is important to bear in
mind that Philip, only recently converted, had had little opportunity to develop his knowledge of Catholic doctrine, so that
reading this document would have brought him clarification
on several contentious points, including the defence of the
canon of Scripture against the ravages of Protestantism (1st
Reason), the true presence of Christ in the Blessed Sacrament,
and other controversies that have pitted Protestantism against
Catholicism.

> And so they behave in every controversy which we
> start. On infused grace, on inherent justice, on the visible
> Church, on the necessity of Baptism, on Sacraments and
> Sacrifice, on the merits of the good, on hope and fear,
> on the difference of guilt in sins, on the authority of
> Peter, on the keys, on vows, on the evangelical counsels,
> on other such points, we Catholics have cited and
> discussed Scripture texts not a few, and of much weight,
> everywhere in books, in meetings, in churches, in the
> Divinity School: they have eluded them. (2nd Reason)

Other arguments that Philip would have encountered concerned the historical nature of the one, true Church which is
affirmed as distinct from the diversity of Protestantism (3rd
Reason), and the authority of the Councils and the Church
Fathers futilely challenged by Protestant minds since these
give the greatest defence possible of Catholic doctrines (4th,
5th and 6th Reasons). In summary, it seems eminently plausi-
ble that Philip reached his conclusions about the authenticity of
the Catholic faith based at least in part on the heroic example
and scholarly written testimony of Edmund Campion.

THE ENGLISH CARDINAL

Cardinal William Allen, a generation older than Philip, had been forced into exile for his Catholic faith and had established a seminary at Ghent in Flanders for the training of priests for the English mission. Before his imprisonment, Philip evidently read Cardinal Allen's recent work on the Catholic cause,[2] since he gave a copy to his brother William to help him come to a decision about his reconciliation to the Catholic Church (AM, p. 20). In this work, Cardinal Allen details the persecution suffered by Catholic priests and laity in England. He even compares their lot to that of the early Christians, and in this he parallels the accounts of Eusebius referred to below. It was to Cardinal Allen that Philip wrote to seek his advice when he was contemplating leaving the country, so the apostolic activities of the Cardinal abroad would have been well known to him.

A well-informed observer of the English scene, Cardinal Allen provided a portrait of the Catholic community being gradually stifled by unjust and illegal persecution. Accused of treason, the priests and other martyrs were in reality condemned for holding to their faith. The existing laws relating to treasonable offences, which dated from the time of Edward III, did not give grounds for their trials, but instead legal measures were specifically instituted by the Elizabethan regime making it an offence, for example, to be a priest. And yet Cardinal Allen points out that the authorities declared that no one was to be condemned simply on a religious charge. In other words, everything had to be done to make it seem as if there was treason when in fact there was nothing in the martyrs' lives that could be considered treasonable according to established English law. Indeed, most of the priests arraigned had not encountered their supposed co-conspirators before their trials, and this was certainly true of Edmund Campion, who had

---

[2]   W. Allen, *A True, Sincere and Modest Defence of English Catholics that Suffer for their Faith both at home and abroad, against a False, Seditious and Slanderous Libel, entitled 'The Execution of Justice in England'* (Rheims, 1584).

spent eight years in Prague immediately before returning to England and was brought to trial less than a year later.

A WORK ON THE ROSARY AND THE 'LITTLE OFFICE OF THE BLESSED VIRGIN MARY'

The Arundel manuscript reports that, in the first letter he was able to write to his wife from the Tower, Philip requested her to procure him two works of Marian spirituality, a book on the Rosary and the *Little Office of the Blessed Virgin Mary*. These books would have had no little influence on Philip's spiritual life. This can be judged, for example, from the fact that he was known to have a special devotion to the Rosary and to have kept his beads with him when he had to forego all other spiritual exercises through his extreme weakness as he lay dying. Oddly, in one sense, Philip had greater freedom to pray the Rosary in the Tower, since outside prison its very possession would have been taken as justification for criminal proceedings.

Gradually Philip must have shifted his emphasis from mere reading to making of his studies a spiritual exercise. He increasingly turned his attention to God. He became familiar with the *Little Office* and the Rosary. He meditated on the themes he discovered in his reading, including the Scriptures. More and more this took over his life and became his solace. It had long been common for lay people to pray the *Little Office of the Blessed Virgin Mary* as a shorter version of the Divine Office. Following this practice, Philip would have come to know the psalms and readings associated with the *Little Office* and these would have harmonised well with his praying of the Rosary with its fifteen mysteries connected with the lives of Jesus and the Blessed Virgin. While it is not known if Philip possessed a Catholic bible,[3] there is plenty of internal evidence from his writing that he had substantial acquaintance with the New Testament, such as his following the Book of Revelation in his

---

[3]   He had in fact inherited a Protestant Bible from his father, but he made no use of it.

references to the Blessed Virgin in his meditation on heaven in his long poem on the four last things.

THE MARTYRS OF THE EARLY CHURCH

We learn from the Arundel manuscript that Philip read 'Eusebius', that is Eusebius of Caesaria, known as the Father of Church History, who lived from *c.* 260 to *c.* 340. The work most likely to have been available to Philip is *The History of the Church*, 'in which, as he signify'd unto Fr Southwell, he found exceeding comfort for the confirmation of his Faith by beholding there how the Church was in her infancy' (AM, p. 107). Eusebius' work, being rather verbose, is not a very readable text, but with its amalgam of vignettes from Church history it stands as one of the most authoritative recordings of events in the post-apostolic Church up to the time of the Emperor Constantine. What is notable about the work, however, is its confirmation of the holiness of the Christian people and the persecution they endured from regimes and emperors who hated the Church. Philip might well have gained 'exceeding comfort' purely of a spiritual kind from the account of the martyrdom of Polycarp by burning, and the bravery he showed by the faith expressed in his final speech.

> Father of your beloved Son Jesus Christ, through whom we have received knowledge of you, the God of angels and of powers and of the whole creation, and of the entire race of the righteous who live in your presence, I bless you that you have deemed me worthy of this day and hour, that I might receive a portion in the number of the martyrs, in the cup of Christ, unto the resurrection of eternal life, both of soul and body, in the immortality of the Holy Spirit. (Book IV, ch. 15)

This is but one of a large number of cases of the fate of martyrs to be found in Eusebius' *History*. Was Philip encouraged by such a history to see that the Church was inevitably under persecution from God's enemies, and how a parallel could be drawn with his own times? The deaths of Polycarp or of Justin

Martyr could be compared with that of the martyr-confessor Edmund Campion in the very recent past. The book also contains comments on the lives of holy men such as Origen, their devotion to prayer, fasting and the study of the Scriptures (Book VIII, ch. 8), and it ends with a lengthy panegyric to God's mercy to his faithful people pronounced at a Church assembly following the ending of the persecutions (Book X, ch. 4), and a consolatory account of the imperial decrees with which the Emperor Constantine established the rights and freedoms of the Church and its members (Book X, ch. 5). Certainly, the story of the conversion of Constantine provided a metaphor for the hopes of Catholics like Philip in the Elizabethan era.

A SPIRITUAL GUIDE

The Arundel manuscript also mentions the work of Fray Luís de Granada, a Spanish spiritual writer, though there is no evidence as to which of his books reached Philip. Most likely is it that Philip read his *La Guía de Pecadores* (The Sinners' Guide).[4] This work, directed at both clergy and laity, proposes patterns of behaviour for Christians and offers remedies against dangers of the world. This seems to be the kind of work that Philip valued, being quite similar in focus to Lanspergius' *Epistle*, to be discussed below, and which would have reinforced his own enduring preoccupation with spiritual combat. It is of particular interest that Fray Luís's book includes four chapters (chapters 7 to 10) concerned with the four last things, which is the subject of Philip's major piece of writing, a poem that is to be explored in the following chapter.

A PRIEST WHO BEFRIENDED HIM
AND BROUGHT HIM COMFORT

From a chapter that was omitted from the Arundel manuscript, but afterwards recovered by Fr Newdigate SJ,[5] we learn of

---

4   L. de Granada, *La Guía de Pecadores* (Lisbon, 1556).
5   C. A. Newdigate, 'A New Chapter in the Life of Bl. Robert Southwell

the circumstances that led to Fr Robert Southwell's coming to
Countess Anne's household, and how he developed a friend-
ship both with the Countess and with her imprisoned husband
to whom he addressed several letters of comfort and advice:

> The Earle at that time was prisoner in the Tower; and
> about two years after, through the malice of his enemies,
> and unjust accusations of some others suborned or set on
> by them, he fell into such troubles, dangers and occasions
> of sorrow and affliction, as necessarily required both
> comfort and advice. For the which he having frequent
> recourse to Fr Southwell by letters conveyed secretly,
> found both of them in such solid and abundant manner
> that he remained no less satisfied than thankful for them.

We learn that Philip read several letters from Robert, later
published in a collection entitled *An Epistle of Comfort*, as well
as an *Epistle* to console him on the death of his sister, Margaret
Sackville, with a beautiful poem at its conclusion including
the line 'Of Howard's stem a glorious branch is dead' (AM, p.
120). There were also letters exchanged between Robert and
Philip on other matters, of which some extracts have been
preserved and are referred to below.

'THE TRIUMPHS OVER DEATH'[6]

It must have touched Philip to receive such a letter concerning his sister's death from someone whom he only knew by
repute, but whose devotion he could not mistake since the
writer was a priest living in his wife's household and caring
for his family. Robert Southwell begins by saying how much
grief he must feel at his sister's untimely death, but with the
consolation that she was a person of great virtue in her life,
resolute in her death, and true to her faith and to her husband.

> I doubt not but that Spirit, whose nature is love, and
> whose name is comforter, as he knows of your grief,

SJ', *The Month* 157 (1931), pp. 246–54.
6   R. Southwell, 'The Triumphs over Death', in *Southwell's Works*, ed.
     W. J. Walter (London: Keating & Co., 1822).

so has he slaved it with supplies of grace, . . . I thought
good to show you, by proof, that you carry not your
cares alone. (p. 89)

He offers the consolation to Philip that his sister's fate is a
blissful one:

you still float in a troublesome sea, and you find it by
experience a sea of dangers: how then can it pity you
to see your sister on shore, and so safely landed in so
blissful a harbour?' (p. 118)

'AN EPISTLE OF COMFORT'[7]

Far more significant, however, would have been the letters
comprising the *Epistle of Comfort* written principally to Philip
by Fr Robert Southwell, seeking to bring him encouragement
and consolation in his sufferings as one of the Catholics being
persecuted for their faith at the time. The Arundel manuscript
confirms that the *Epistle* contributed much to Philip's solace
by quoting letters from Philip to the priest where he expresses
his appreciation and gratitude (AM, p. 134). Shining through
the *Epistle* are the sincerity of Robert Southwell's beliefs and
concerns, his deep knowledge of the faith and of scripture and
the beauty of his language and sentiments. Added to these
qualities, he showed an invincible courage when he was facing
his execution not many years later, and the gist of his speech
from the scaffold must have reached Philip in the eight months
between Southwell's execution and his own death.

Fr Southwell finds reasons to console Philip, contrasting
his lot with the blessings being prepared for him in heaven.
He commends him as defending the 'only true and Catholic
religion'. He rehearses arguments against the Reformers. He
reassures him of the certain hope that he has of victory. He

---

[7]   R. Southwell, 'An Epistle of comfort to the reverent priests, and to
    the honorable, worshipful and others of the lay sort, restrained in
    durance for the Catholic Faith', in *Southwell's Works* , ed. Walter, pp.
    125–99.

should be consoled by the thought that he is sheltered by his imprisonment from so much blasphemy and temptation. The main message of the *Epistle* was to encourage Philip to see himself as one of those called to suffer with and for Christ, and to urge him to take solace from this.

> You defend a Church founded by Christ, enlarged by his apostles, impugned by none but infidels and enemies of the truth; whose doctrine can be derived from no late author, convicted of no novelty, afflicted with no variableness, change of contrariety, in essential points of belief. (p. 148)

With persuasive arguments, he urges Philip to endurance to the point of martyrdom. If he is to die he will have a martyr's reward.

> Death of itself to the good is not so odious, but that, for infinite reasons, they have rather cause to wish it than to avoid it, and motives to desire it rather than to fear it. (pp. 163–4)

Philip can resolutely face martyrdom, because he has the example of so many before him who trusted in God's promise of life.

> Consider the whole multitude and glorious host of martyrs whose torments have been exquisite, bloody, and with all kinds of extremity, and yet their minds were undaunted and strong, and their agonies always ended in triumph and victory. (pp. 171–2)

The importance of the example of those who suffer for the true faith cannot be exaggerated.

> Our prisons preach; our punishments convert; and even our dead corpses are able to confound heresy. (p. 194)

Robert Southwell is so enthralled with the prospect facing Philip that he would wish the same for himself since it foretells such an eternal reward.

> Joy in your happiness, and pray that God may accept us also, and promote us to the like comfort; always remembering with yourselves that 'this light and

momentary tribulation will work in you an eternal weight of glory'.

Philip can look forward to death as a martyr: 'Where the conscience is clear death is looked for without fear; yea, desired with delight, accepted with devotion.' Embracing death is the principal act of obedience since Christ was obedient unto death. These martyrs will one day be honoured. This prophecy has not yet been fully realised but undoubtedly lives on in the hearts of St Robert and St Philip.

The authorities are in effect creating saints who will be revered in time to come.

> We have now, God be thanked! Such martyr-makers in authority as mean, if they have their will, to make saints enough to furnish all our churches with treasure, when it shall please God to restore them to their true honours, and doubt not but that they, or their posterity, shall see the very prisons of execution become places of reverence and devotion, and the scattered bones of those who in this cause have suffered, though now thought unworthy of Christian burial, then shrined in gold, and held in the greatest respect. (p. 197)

A LETTER FROM ROBERT SOUTHWELL

One of the last letters from Robert to Philip broaches plainly the likelihood of his martyrdom, which Robert encourages him to await as 'the highest honour'.

> Martyrdom confers the highest honour on any man: to you it will bring a double palm, for you will be able to say with the psalmist, *Praestitisti decori meo virtutem* (You gave strength to my beauty), since you have crowned nobility with the cross of Christ.[8]

An echo of this letter is found in a consolatory poem by Robert, *I Die without Desert*, which it is generally agreed was written about Philip's fate and which he very likely read.

---

[8]   Published by H. More, *Historia Provinciae Anglicanae* (1660), p. 186.

Thus Fortune's favours still are bent to flight.
Thus worldly bliss in final bale doth end,
Thus virtue still pursued is with spight.
But let my fate, though rueful, none offend.
God doth, sometimes, first crop the sweetest flower,
And leaves the weed, till Time do it devour.[9]

Apart from the wisdom that Philip was able to draw from the authors he studied, however, it needs to be said that he must surely have benefited from an infusion of divine knowledge, not of doctrine or of knowledge of the Church but an opening up to vistas of the interior life suited to his culture and intellect. This will become more apparent with the next chapter's examination of his written work. There is no need to exaggerate his personal holiness since everything he gained was gift, for we do not make ourselves holy. God, however, calls all to holiness and some, like St Philip, have responded more humbly and fruitfully to his call.

[9] See Appendix A for the complete poem in its original spelling.

✢ 3 ✢

Philip's Interior Life Reflected in his Writings

N O ONE SEEMS TO HAVE SUBJECTED St Philip's writings to close examination even though they accounted for such a significant part of his time in the Tower. The mainly pamphlet-style, biographical literature on him hardly alludes to this aspect of his life. Yet the fact is that in his writing he was examining his own heart rather than compiling a spiritual guide for others like some famous writers of letters from prison. He appears to have seen his confinement as reparation and penance for his own and perhaps for others' lives. Since, because of his seclusion in the Tower, we have little direct information on Philip's interior life, reviewing these written works provides an indispensable way to access and interpret his inner experience, his motives, insights, resolutions, and his understanding of the meaning and relevance of his imprisonment for his faith and his life, both before and during his long vigil.

Philip never had the chance to become a scholar like his contemporaries Edmund Campion and Robert Southwell. With all due respect to his two years spent at Cambridge, he did well to be accomplished enough in Latin to be able to translate the work of Lanspergius that will be examined shortly. We cannot look to him for polished prose or verse. Instead we have the testimony of a resolute, tenacious faith, often grim in its consciousness of sin and the need for redemption, which no doubt reflects the harshness of his treatment at the hands of his jailers and his isolation from the living Church and its liturgy. His writings echo the basics of the faith; they are Christ-centred and sustained with an immovable trust in God. He is not like those seminarians at the Venerabile, or English College, in Rome, who were reported as heading joyfully to martyrdom. While he did aspire to die for Christ, it was undoubtedly with a heavy heart, a heart already inured to pain and separation from the companionship of family and like-minded people, both recusant Catholics and people to whom he could carry the Gospel. Nonetheless, we can look to his writing to find in it the expression of his faith and the witness it bears to Christ.

BEFORE HIS IMPRISONMENT

The letter to the Queen, 11–14 April 1585 (AM, pp. 31–51) The principal document that we have that was written by Philip before his trial, and which throws light on his spiritual commitment and life, is the letter he wrote to Queen Elizabeth before attempting to flee the country in April 1585. In this lengthy letter, Philip first of all declares his intent to explain his situation and protest his innocence of any crime of treason with the hope of a fair hearing. He feels he has been punished by being confined to his house for fifteen weeks without any cause being given. He realises that he is in some danger because of his reconciliation with the Catholic Church, but he makes a resolute confession of faith, despite all the dangers he was in from his enemies:

> [I] resolved whilst I had oportunitie to take that course which might be sure to save my soule from the danger of shipwracke although my body were subject to the peril of misfortune. And ever since the time that I followed and performed that good intent of mine, though I perceyved somwhat more danger to my estate, yet I humbly thank God I have found a great deale more quiett in my minde. And at this present I have occasion to thinke my most mortall enemyes my chiefest friends; nay I have most just occasion to esteeme my past troubles as my greatest felicity. For both of them were (though indirectly) means to lead me to the course, which bringeth perfitt quyetness, and onely procureth eternall happyness.

He records that he reached the decision to leave the country, 'and abide in some other place where I myght live without danger to my conscience, without offence to your majesty', but that he did not wish to do so without explaining why, so as to avoid misunderstanding of his motives, affirming that 'I would not have taken this course if I might have stayed still in England without danger to my soule and perill to my life.' He returns to his underlying purpose and hope for understanding from the Queen:

> And though the losse of temporale commodityes be soe greivous to flesh and bloud, as I could not desire to lyve if I were not comforted by the hope of eternall happynes in another world and with the remembrance of his mercy, for whom I endure all this (who endured ten thousand times more for me) yet I assure your Majesty that your displeasure should be more unpleasant unto me than the bitterness of all my other losses, and a greater greife than my greatest misfortunes are besides.

We see the care Philip takes to anticipate any complaint that the Queen might harbour against him by assuring her of his loyalty. The only offence he acknowledges is to have taken measures to safeguard the integrity of his own conscience in his loyalty to his Catholic faith. This is the very same position taken by St Thomas More before his execution: 'I am the King's good servant, but God's first'.

HIS WRITING IN THE TOWER

The Inscriptions

Unfortunately, we do not know the order of composition of all Philip's writings, but he did record the date of the textual inscriptions he left carved in his cell. While in the Beauchamp Tower he made three carvings:
- A crucifix, then two textual inscriptions:
- *Sicut peccati causa vinciri opprobrium est, ita e contra, pro Christo custodiae vincula sustinere, maxima gloria est. Arundell, 26 of May 1587.* (As it is a disgrace to be in bonds for sin, so, on the con-

trary, it is the highest glory to be bound and imprisoned for Christ's sake.)

• *Quanto plus afflictiones pro Christo in hoc saeculo, tanto plus gloriae cum Christo in futuro. Arundell June 22 1587.* (The more affliction for Christ in this world, the more glory with Christ in the next.)

In spite of being only fifteen words long, it is undeniable that the greatest clue we have to Philip's state of mind is the later inscription he carved on the mantelpiece of his cell. These two statements of hope sum up Philip's life. They are of course scriptural, recalling words of St Paul which he most probably had in mind, prompted possibly by Fr Southwell's use of this same text in one of his letters (see above, pp. 20–1): For this slight momentary affliction is preparing us for an eternal weight of glory beyond all measure, because we look not at what can be seen but at what cannot be seen (cf. 2 Cor 4: 17–18).

Philip must have intended these defiant carvings to stand as a testimony to his faith and hope, something that he was leaving for posterity and which he did not intend ever to gainsay. They are a golden testimony to the saint's spiritual life. They show that he was reconciled to his death, that he even desired it. In his poem on the Passion, to be commented upon below, he speaks of the graces Christ's Cross wins for us. He carried his own cross to the end. He was stripped of his title and possessions and yet he forgave those who made themselves his enemies. He made no complaint and Christ was triumphant in his life.

An Epistle of the Lord Jesus Christ

The major piece of writing that we have of Philip's, dating most probably from some considerable time into his imprisonment, is not of his own composition but is his translation from the Latin of a spiritual manual in the tradition of *The Imitation of Christ*, by a German Charterhouse monk, John Justus Lanspergius, who died in 1539. The work is very substantial, some 100,000 words in translation, and is presented as words coming from Jesus himself. Even if we do not know how it came into Philip's hands, it is nevertheless clear that it was consciously selected as a significant text, both for his own interest and as worth the time and effort of translating for others who would read it in English. And, more importantly for our purposes, although the *Epistle* involves some demanding and detailed exegesis, we must engage with it as a key source of insight into the saint's interior life.

Such an *Epistle*, addressed to a community of nuns by a monk, might be thought to be of limited concern to ordinary Christians, especially in later times. Nonetheless, the spiritual principle of loving submission to the will of God affirmed in the *Epistle* speaks not only to Philip's contemporaries but also to modern Christians who are committed to seeking amendment of life and holiness. If, therefore, we want to better understand the motivation and the path to holiness followed by St Philip so as to benefit from his wisdom and inspiration for our times, the *Epistle* is an indispensable source. This is not to say that he would have formulated his thoughts in the same way as Lanspergius, since he did not have the formation of a contemplative monk, but there are obvious parallels between the concerns of the original author and the preoccupations that must have dogged Philip during his cloistering in the Tower as the setting for developing his own relationship to God.

He knew he was to follow Christ to Calvary, but he did not see himself as the virtuous one leaving the sinners behind. He was a sinner who would have been shirking his responsibility if he did not own up and take the consequences. He was a person who himself needed the inspiration of Lanspergius. He was the sinner Christ was redeeming. He was the one who had to fear God's judgement. And the only way he could prepare himself to face his judge was by humbling himself, being obedient, even to those who had shown themselves to be his enemies, submitting to the strictures of their system of denunciation, injustice, and condemnation to endure whatever fate was to come as his offering in repentance to the Almighty.

It would not be feasible to follow the 35 chapters of Lanspergius' *Epistle* with detailed commentary, especially as they do not appear to have an inherent sequence. Instead we will have recourse to an overall structure and ordering to help discern Philip's spiritual priorities. Essentially, the author holds up to us a mirror of the spiritual life in which we can recognise, on the one hand, our own experience of being placed in particular circumstances by a mixture of personal determination what God wills and what he permits and, on the other, our receiving the call to make a positive response to God despite our human weaknesses. The chapters of the *Epistle* can then, for simplicity's sake, be divided into these two categories: those that refer to the givens of life, and those that refer to the development of the soul's relationship with God.

The first category, which we can call the enforced circumstances, has many elements, especially since human beings enjoy free-will and do not always find it easy to bend to a spiritual discipline. They include biographical features, personal characteristics and talents, factors in one's upbringing, events, pressures and impositions of public life, and also God's action in our lives.

The second category, the soul's response to God, can be seen as the interpretation of God's call and attempts to resolve the demands it makes in an evolving relationship with God. Also, it consists rather in an interior response than in its practical effect, such as in attending Mass, receiving the sacraments, or saying specific prayers. Thus, it includes love of God and neighbour, virtues such as humility, perseverance and obedience to God's will, and giving God his due through love, praise and thanksgiving.

The general tenor of the *Epistle* The foundation of the spirituality endorsed in the *Epistle* is love, God's love for man and man's love for God. This is distinct from the love of the world, which is essentially a love of self. It is also the daily reality that Philip is living: what goes on in God's heart and in his own heart. We are to show love for God by obeying his commandments, that is aligning our will with his and living in his will rather than following our own will and wilfulness in sin. Part of this obedience is to trust that all that happens to us is allowed by God, whether contentment or adversity, and for this God should be thanked and praised. God allows us to encounter hardship so that we can share his sufferings and his Cross and merit an eternal reward. He may also send us joys as consolations so that we are not tried beyond our strength.

Introduction The Introduction to the *Epistle* laments the way that the soul is so attached to the world that it neglects to use the precious time it has to honour and serve God, when it needs to be poor in spirit and humble, contemplating the miseries of Christ's life so as to rejoice as much in suffering as in consolations by doing his will always. Philip must have reflected on how apposite this was for his own life, where he had spent so many years in worldly pursuits, as the Arundel manuscript attests, hardly thinking at all of God or of his own salvation (*Epistle*, pp. 1–22).

The enforced circumstances By his removal from public life and his incarceration, Philip had to endure isolation from human company and yet learn to survive retaining his faith and trust in God. It is hard to imagine how he could have done this without taking to heart Lanspergius' advice on contemplative prayer and openness to God's consolations.

> Solitariness, silence, purity, and simplicity of heart, do prepare a place for me to dwell in. Keep thyself, therefore, withdrawn from all creatures, in silence and quietness of heart. Do not seek consolation from creatures . . . remain with me always alone, recollected within thy own soul, and withdrawn not only from all other creatures, but even from thine own self; that is, from all liking to procure thine own pleasure, from all care to seek thine own commodity, and from all desire to serve thy own appetite. (Ch. 4)

God does not admit of rivals, so we are to turn from the idols of other rewards and pleasures. That is, we have to forsake the world's temptations and delights if we are to truly honour, respect, love and serve God and enjoy his consolations and peace. Philip lived this commitment to the utmost. He turned from a worldly life to one of enforced reclusion, and he maintained this stance to the end, even foregoing the possibility of seeing his wife and his son before his death when to do so he would have been required to attend a Protestant service against his conscience.

> If thou wilt obtain me wholly, O Soul, thou must of necessity, and altogether cast off thyself. Thou must

submit and resign over thyself to extreme poverty, and the want of all temporal commodities and consolations, for obtaining of me, who am the chiefest and greatest good. (Ch. 35)

Philip would surely have read as an encouragement to hope the following passage from Lanspergius, in which the consolations of heaven are contrasted with the miseries of earthly rewards, in words ascribed to Jesus.

If they delight in love, why love they not me, whose love is chaste, pure, holy, and simple; who am an object always offered to their eyes, of infinite amiableness, being essentially good in myself, being a pure good, unmixed, being the chiefest and sovereign good, where the reward of love also is unspeakable delight, and most blessed eternity? Whereas the love of the world, on the contrary part, doth breed nothing in thy soul but unquietness, bitterness, distraction, repentance, and heaviness. (Ch. 32)

Even a saint would have to admit that it is not easy to reject the world's allurements on account of pride, the desire for self-sufficiency, and weakness in resisting temptation. However, through grace, the Christian can become humble, obedient and loving. God makes radical demands upon the soul, including discipline of the senses so as to please him in all that we think, say or do, not seeking delights in food and drink for their own sake but only consuming what is necessary for the body to be able to function well. Moreover, the Lord is portrayed as saying that we should never complain at our sufferings but only think of those he endured for us. Such was Philip's uncomplaining endurance of his rigorous confinement with so little comfort or consolation.

For as long as thou thinkest thyself to be wronged, as long as thou complainest, and dost believe that thou hast received any injury, thou art not clearly purged of self-love. For thou shouldst not, in truth, take anything for an injury, but that wrong which is done unto me. (Ch. 31)

Lanspergius advises the sisters, and by extension all his readers, to submit willingly and joyfully to God's will in whatever circumstances he chooses to place them. It was surely the secret of Philip's sanctity that he was able to decide for a prolonged sacrifice. While it might be said that he had little choice but to be obedient, yet resentment and bitterness could have shown themselves unless he disciplined himself very strictly.

> Be ready at all times without any choice, without any difference and without any murmuring in thy heart, to receive for the fulfilling of my pleasure, adversity as willingly as prosperity, both temporally and eternally, desiring always this only thing, that thou mayest ever be in all respects according to my will. (Ch. 22)

But how do we know and become what God wills us to be? We are to pray for God's assistance to embrace the cross for his sake, to be obedient to his will, to live a life of self-denial and to be poor in spirit. Philip finds himself obliged to surrender his own will to the authorities but, by his free choice, also to God. We learn from the Arundel manuscript that he practised self-denial by fasting, thus repudiating his former lifestyle with its wealth and luxuries. The Christian is also to offer forgiveness together with prayers for any who have given offence. From all that we know of Philip he retained a kind, forgiving and courteous manner until the end, when he forgave the Tower superintendent for his habitual severity.

> Endeavour, therefore, to excuse every man, and to do them good by thy prayers, benefits, and all the pleasures that lieth in thy power. And upon such as thou canst bestow no other benefit, seek to mitigate their sorrow with thy courteous behaviour, thy sweet speech, or any other means that thou art able. (Ch. 26)

Truly to imitate God is to imitate the humility of Christ. We have nothing of which to be proud, and therefore humility especially becomes us. Hardship was Philip's lot; the discomfort, cold, poor diet and mistreatment he received could be looked at as so many ways in which he imitated Christ by humbly and obediently submitting to the truth of the faith and to God's will. The ultimate humiliation for Philip was for his case to be ignored, rejected and despised by the Queen and her ministers.

> Desire of me, with tears and sighs, perfect humility, that
> by it thou mayest delight to lie hidden and unknown,
> to be contemned, and held in no estimation. (Ch. 17)

We are to trust that all that happens to us is allowed by God,
whether contentment or adversity, and for that God should be
thanked and praised. We do not know if in his prayers Philip
praised God for all that had befallen him, but he accepted
his lot and tried to make the best of it by not complaining
of his trials. God allows us to encounter hardship so that we
can share his Cross and his glory. Philip committed himself
wholeheartedly to Christ and knew that he could trust God
for his eventual reward, as he plainly stated in the inscriptions
he left in his cell.

> Wheresoever, therefore, that I go, desire to accompany
> me; whatsoever I do, study to imitate me; whatsoever I
> suffer, be ready to suffer with me; and if by any occasion
> thou feelest tribulation, rejoice in it, because by it thou
> art made like unto me. (Ch. 15)

The Soul's Response to God Although the note struck by
the German monk may appear to be exceptionally ascetic
and mournful, this tenor is not sustained in the passages that
concern the soul's response to God. Here the emphasis is on
the blessings of union with Christ and the saints. The first
blessing is fervent prayer. We know of Philip's attachment to
the Mass, and we can take as further evidence of his Catholic
Eucharistic faith the words of Lanspergius that he translated:

> But because thou mayest be inflamed with a greater
> reverence, love, and desire, towards this Blessed
> Sacrament, I assure thee that, without all doubt, my
> body is there sacramentally delivered unto thee, to be
> received under the form of bread. Wherefore, seeing it
> is the same body, which I now carry glorified in heaven;
> seeing it is no other, nor any like unto it, but even the
> very same; and seeing I carry not a body which is dead
> nor without blood, it followeth of necessity that, together
> in the same body, there must be also contained my soul,
> my blood, my graces, and my virtues. (Ch. 13)

Philip would also have had the advice of Lanspergius in mind when he composed himself in prayer, as when the Carthusian says:

> have thine eye so fixed upon eternity in this present world as if thou wert quite separated from it, and clearly delivered out of it, beholding all the things in this world afar off, as those things which thou hast wholly forsaken, and from which thou hast clearly weaned thyself. Think that thou art alone with me, and that I am with thee, and as if there were no other creature present with thee. (Ch. 35)

It is this discipline that Philip now had to learn in the isolation of his prison cell, to surrender any vestiges of longing for his former life and to transfer all his loving and longing to God alone. This was the reality that Philip was now called to live, and this love should lead him to abandon any resentment he feels at the injustices he has suffered, and instead to praise and thank God for these very adversities.

> For there is nothing that doth so lively resemble the state of the blessed happiness in the world to come, as the cheerful and delightful voice of those which do praise my name. (Ch. 33)

Philip devoted hours of each day to prayer. He attached great importance to the Rosary offered in honour of the Virgin Mary, and we know that he also prayed the *Little Office of the Blessed Virgin Mary*.

> Salute my Mother often and zealously, with thy fervent prayers; and honour her ever with all reverence and a principal devotion, by seeking diligently to imitate both her life and her virtue. (Ch. 11)

The Christian then is not to trust in himself but in Christ who can not only strengthen us in our trials but even take on the burdens we carry, provided we remain poor in spirit.

> Faint not, therefore, in thy courage, for thou shalt overcome all things by settling thy whole trust in my mercy. Have confidence in me, and thou shalt find that I will make these crosses light for thee, and help thee

myself to bear part of the burthen ... But this trust in
me can never be without a distrust in thyself, and both
these graces are only obtained by poverty of spirit,
which is a most precious jewel. (Ch. 2)

Lanspergius proposes that we stake everything on the mercy
of God despite all trials. Great spiritual perseverance seems
to have characterised Philip's life in the Tower. But he was
confident that this was all to a good purpose. The last decade
of his life was essentially a preparation for death. We can be
sure that looking back on the hardships of his life Philip must
find that they counted for little in comparison with the joys of
eternal life. He must wish that people would learn from his
experience how one comes through afflictions to glory.

I look for also a firm hope, and an assured trust in my
mercy, and a constancy in thee, that will neither be
overcome with any assault, nor yet wearied with any
travail ... the more thy good will is tempted by adversity,
and the more faithful it is found, and the more patient
it is in bearing of crosses, and such things as resist it,
the more glorious the crown is which I have laid up to
reward it. (Ch. 6)

And, finally, for his consolation and his inspiration, Philip will
have contemplated the words:

Go, therefore, out of thyself, and forsake thyself, that
I only may possess thee, and that thou only mayest
possess me. This is a short time which is present, but
that which followeth is without all limitation of time
and eternal, without any end. (Conclusion)

PHILIP'S POETIC WORKS

Philip mainly chooses for his poems the familiar topics of his
time. It is as if he wanted to make their subject-matter his own
by re-working the themes that had so preoccupied Catholics
since the Middle Ages. Guiney has produced a rich and edify-
ing collection of recusants' poems, including some by Philip.
They offer a wide variety of subjects, not all of them religious,

but including devotional or pious works treating of Christ's passion, Our Lady, the Eucharist, regret for sin, especially those of youth, the joys of heaven, and the trials being undergone by the Catholic faithful.[1]

A Foure-fould Meditation, of the foure last things[2]

The most substantial of Philip's poems, on the four last things, is especially relevant to our study, since it is a meditation on death, judgement, hell and heaven written while he was under sentence of death, probably towards the end of 1587 and therefore just after he carved his inscriptions. The earliest edition of the work ascribes the poem to Robert Southwell, but the subsequent discovery of manuscript copies made Philip's authorship clear.[3] The probable dating of the poem as preceding his work on Lanspergius is significant, since this would likely mean that it reflects more Philip's own thinking. The lengthy poem (119 stanzas of six lines each), with its concentration on the horrors of an unprepared death contrasted with the possibility of a blessed eternity, was in the tradition of writings on the four last things that greatly preoccupied medieval and pre-Reformation writers.[4] We can only speculate on the precise motives that led Philip to compose this poem, but it was evidently intended as a warning from someone who sees he could so easily have taken the broad rather than the narrow path. The way he chose involved pursuing acts of penitence, but the ultimate focus is on the attainment of heaven that is promised to the righteous. He kept trying to put this into words to convey how sinners deserve damnation and would be justly damned were it not for God's mercy. No one has a right to salvation, and he did not think that he did. He sees that it is better to say where the praise really belongs,

[1]   L. I. Guiney, *Recusant Poets* (London: Sheed & Ward, 1939).
[2]   *Foure-fould Meditation, of the foure last things viz. 1 2 3 4 of the Houre of Death. Day of Judgement. Paines of Hell. Joys of Heaven. Shewing the estate of the Elect and Reprobate* (first published 1606).
[3]   Pollen and MacMahon, *Unpublished Documents*, p. 326.
[4]   E. Duffy, *The Stripping of the Altars: Traditional Religion in England c. 1400–c. 1580* (Newhaven: Yale University Press, 1992), ch. 9.

to the merciful Father and to Jesus Christ who suffered for our redemption.

While he was following a tradition in meditating on the four last things, he was also adapting it to his own circumstances. He was aware that he needed to make amends for his earlier life so as not to face an adverse judgement from God. Perhaps he leaned over backwards to paint the picture of a grievous sinner, but he saw that every sin is a serious insult to Almighty God, and it is the sinner he has in mind, not the one who has no need of repentance. He wanted to help save souls, the ones who risked damnation on account of unrepented sins. This is not questioning the mercy of God, far from it, since even saints need his mercy, but sinners are in more desperate need. In showing the fate of an unrepentant sinner he is warning all that the time for repentance is while life continues, before it is too late to change one's heart to come to contrition. If the picture of death is not sufficient to warn people that this life is over in a breath, then the reminder of God's judgement reinforces the point. Life on earth ends, and then comes an inevitable judgement. When his meditation dwells on hell he is merely pressing the point home. Judgement is real, and irreversible. Heaven is unimaginable bliss, so he does what he can to portray it, but he knows that no eye has seen, and no ear has heard the blessedness and delights for those who come to enjoy the presence of Almighty God in his heavenly Kingdom.

Death Alone in his cell and under sentence of death, Philip is impelled to ponder the four last things. Never knowing if and when the sentence will be carried out, he can hardly be imagined not to be thinking of death, and of his own in particular. On death, he strikes a gruesome note, as in the following verse:

> *Thy voice doth yield a hoarse and hollow sound,*
> *Thy dying head doth greedy seem to sleep,*
> *Thy senses all with horror doth abound,*
> *Thy feet doth die, and death doth upward creep:*
> *Thy eyes doth stand, fast set into thine head,*
> *Thy jaws doth fall, and show thee almost dead.* (v. 6)

In this he was following other writers of the time, for they often focussed attention on features of the dying, even decomposing, body. Duffy quotes St Thomas More's rendering of the death throes of a man that was aimed at prompting people to think of their own deaths and inciting them to prepare themselves for judgement (Duffy, p.308).

The poet regrets the errors of his past, the sinful life of a courtier who lived only for his own glory. He does not want to be one of those who die without confessing his sins, repenting and seeking forgiveness from God. The poem constitutes a personal confession insofar as the author identifies himself with the sinner by references to lands, wealth, costly clothes, choice meats, a wife and children, all of which he must leave behind.

> *Thou art not sure one moment for to live,*
> *And at thy death thou leavest all behind,*
> *Thy lands and goods no succour then can give,*
> *Thy pleasures past are crosses to thy mind*
> *Thy friend the world can yield thee no relief*
> *Thy greatest joy will prove thy greatest grief.* (v. 2)

He cares for sinners. There is a comparison between the state to which the soul is called and the heaven that will be lost when sinners leave repentance too late.

> *Now heaven to win no pains thou wouldst refuse,*
> *Nor spare thy goods to ease thy woeful state,*
> *Of all thy sins thou dost thy self accuse,*
> *And call for grace when calling comes too late.* (v. 14)

Judgement He fears the moment when the Book of Life will be opened, and he will be asked to give an account of his every thought, word, deed and omission. Although he has accepted God's grace and has attempted to live a life in conformity to God's will since his conversion, this is but part of what he has received, not what he has himself achieved. All he can hope for is that God, who never goes back on his promises, will receive him as a poor beggar, recognising that he is utterly dependent on him but believing in his mercy as much as his justice. Each soul must face the divine judge:

> *Thou must appear before the Judge on high,*
> *And have reward as thou thy life hast led.* (v. 20)

But woe betide the sinner who excites God's wrath:

> *Behold his throne of glory in the skies,*
> *And see how wrath doth sparkle from his eyes.* (v. 21)

The poet imagines all the ways the dying man might find himself accused without being able to offer any defence against the Lord's reproach that by his sins he was serving the devil rather than Christ who had died for him:

> *Our Lord doth say, 'how couldst thou use me so,*
> *Since I to thee both soul and body gave?*
> *How durst thou seek and serve my mortal foe,*
> *Since I did die thy self from death to save?*
> *I gave thee all, and me thou didst detest,*
> *He gave thee naught, yet wholly thee possest'.* (v. 30)

God's adverse judgement is therefore given as that which the sinner willingly brought on himself:

> *O thankless wretch thou me shalt see no more,*
> *But dwell with him who had thy heart before.* (v. 32)

> *Thy own deserts have made thee his to be,*
> *The choice was thine, no wrong is done to thee.* (v. 33)

In several verses, the devil makes his case to God against the soul (vv. 34–8). The Last Judgement is then portrayed through the fear that spreads across the earth, the signs of disruption in nature, the darkening sun, the falling stars, the mountains moving, the angels sounding their trumpets, and

> *Behold how Christ in glory cometh now,*
> *And in the air appears a flame of fire.* (v. 47)

Hell The punishment of hell is being banished forever from God's sight, a fate the poet cannot imagine without quivering in terror. Yet hell exists, and there are many who may find their way into its fires. Philip himself might wonder what will become of Elizabeth and her courtiers, agents and henchmen who so mistreated him. He cannot himself be their judge or even claim to be better than them. The truth is that he does not know how he might have acted if he had been in their position. God's mercy spared him that, but did he make a return of love to such a merciful God? He cannot presume God's acceptance but can only hope in his mercy.

It has been commented that Philip makes no mention of Purgatory in this poem, but this is not to be taken as suggesting that he did not believe that there was an alternative to hell for those who die not in a state of grace. In his poem on the Passion there is a reference to purging:

> *Graunt that thy going downe to them that did thy sighte desire,*
> *May keep my sowle when I am dead cleane from the purging fire.*

Also, as we shall see, Philip made provision in his will for a chantry, whereby Masses would be offered for souls in Purgatory, and this was a strong statement to a society that had outlawed reference to Purgatory as a *non-biblical* doctrine.

Philip's graphic vision of hell recalls Dante's *Inferno*, with the frightening appearance of demons and the regrets and the sufferings of the damned that are made to fit the sins they committed in life.

> *Lo here the fruit which worldly pleasures bring,*
> *Thy pains agree in measure with thy sin.* (v. 75)

> *Thy greedy mind is punisht here with lack,*
> *thy lecherous arms do ugly fiends embrace.* (v. 76)

> *Thy costly clothes are now made burning flames.*
> *Thy lofty pride hath now a loathsome fall.* (v. 77)

Above all the damned suffer the loss of the sight of God:

> *The pain of sense small torment thou dost find,*
> *When thou this loss dost call unto thy mind.* (v. 79)

Heaven Philip devotes a substantial part of his poem to heaven. The whole poem comprises an act of faith in God, Creator, Redeemer and Holy Spirit, and in the blessings of eternal life in the communion of saints for those who attain paradise. The comparison to Dante's work is again relevant but, as in the case of Dante, hell or the inferno proved easier to depict. The imagination of the poet is necessarily more strained when contemplating the everlasting bliss of paradise, as he says:

> *No eye hath seen what joys the saints obtain,*
> *No ear hath heard what comforts are possest:*
> *No heart can think in what delight they reign,*
> *Nor pen express their happy port of rest* (v. 118)

Heaven is the prospect to which Philip feels drawn with every fibre of his being. For so long he has dreamt of joining the band of martyrs who stood firm for the faith and even wished to die as witnesses to the truth. What were all his prayers if not the evidence of his longing? What was the meaning of his daily sufferings, his stifling of feelings of resentment, complaint or anger at the injustices heaped upon him, and still more of any judgement of his betrayers, if he was not content to leave to the Almighty the judgement and the righting of wrongs? Indeed, it would add to his felicity if he could meet again in the heavenly Kingdom with all those who were the cause of his hardships. That is the prospect that he holds dear, a time when all will be made good, when justice will be restored, when peace will reign, when hostilities will cease, when the Church will be triumphant in glory and God's will is carried through to its merciful conclusion.

There is where he hopes to find a place, however insignificant, from which he can behold in truth what he has sought to witness to by his life on earth. He feels that no one could be more grateful than he for the salvation of his soul, and he knows he cannot compare the pains and torments of the present with the wonders and happiness of eternal life. He anticipates meeting his heavenly Mother to whom he is so devoted, and who must have softened the harshness of his treatment by her consolations. Since he has lived for Christ, he hopes to see his face and to enjoy the vision of God. He will meet again the sainted people who, whether he knew them personally or not, were spiritual guides and counsellors. In short, he will find that the overwhelming experience of paradise makes up for everything in the past and takes him far beyond the prayers he dutifully offered whilst on earth to an encounter with divine reality, the *summum bonum* which he could only access by humble faith.

Philip relies substantially upon the Book of Revelation to evoke heaven's light:

> *Of sun and moon it needeth not the light,*
> *For ever there the Lamb is shining bright* (v. 88)

The river lined with trees gives healing, and the saints are assembled, praising God:

> *They swim in bliss which now shall never cease,*
> *And singing all, his name for ever praise:*
> *Before his throne in white they daily stand,*
> *And carry palms of triumph in their hands.* (v. 9)

He includes a vision of the Virgin Mary, crowned Queen of Heaven, as in Revelation, chapter 12, and proclaims the honour due to Mary:

> *and with stars her head is richly crowned:*
> *In glory she all creatures passeth far:*
> *The moon her shoes, the sun her garments are.* (v. 96)

Reaching the climax of the poem, Philip in several verses describes Christ the Lord appearing in glory sitting at the right hand of the Father, and the saints' beatific vision:

> *They face to face do God Almighty see!*
> *And all in him as in a perfect glass:*
> *No good there is, but there is found to be.*
> *And all delights this vision doth surpass.* (v. 108)

And, finally, the joys of heaven are compared with what the saints have left behind:

> *O blessed joys, which all the souls possess!*
> *O happy fruit, that virtue here hath won!*
> *And in degrees the bodies find no less,*
> *But shine with beams far brighter than the sun:*
> *Not subject now to sickness, grief, or pain,*
> *But glorious all, immortal they remain.* (v. 115)

Despite the tour de force that this poem represents, it may not be unfair to describe Philip as more a versifier than a poet. This is not criticism; it simply means that he sometimes found it easier to express himself in the laconic, expressive mode of a poem than by a logical rationale. We see the latter characteristic in his letters, but for what are perhaps deeper topics he turns to verse. It is possible that the language and expression of poetry offered him a greater opportunity and freedom to record his feelings and the essence of his prayers, and even allowed him a certain distancing from his own pains, while being able to share them with a reader.

It is most likely that Philip was inspired in his poetry, both stylistically and in content, by Robert Southwell, though Robert was far more scholarly, and more intellectually and culturally formed. This shows in the stylistic variety of Robert's writing, the scriptural and classical references in his works, and the varied expression of his writing. Philip was a simpler man who was very focused and straightforward, but who had been captured by the Lord. If we compare Philip's verses with those of Robert on a similar theme we may find different styles, approaches and depth of learning, but the same faith. As an illustration, Robert Southwell begins his poem *Fortune's Falsehood*,[5] following a theme closely related to the four last things, with the enchanting lines:

> *In worldly merriments lurketh much misery,*
> *Fly fortune's subtleties in baits of happiness*
> *Shroud hooks that swallowed without recovery,*
> *Murder the innocent with mortal heaviness.*
>
> . . . . . .
>
> *With fawning flattery death's door she openeth,*
> *Alluring passengers to bloody destiny;*
> *In offers bountiful in proof she beggareth,*
> *Man's ruins regist'ring her false felicity.*

5   R. Southwell, *The Complete Works with Life and Death* (London: D. Stewart, 1876), p. 51.

OTHER POEMS

The Wrackes of Walsingham[6] Philip's authorship of this poem about the misfortune that had befallen Walsingham, the Norfolk shrine of Our Lady that had been ransacked and ruined by the Reformers, has not been universally recognised, but both Duffy and Saward *et al.*, found enough evidence to believe it could be attributed to him, and there is little doubt but that he would have professed the sentiments that the poem expresses.[7] Not only was he the son of a Duke of Norfolk but he is known to have spent time at his Norfolk home in Norwich, and almost certainly saw the ruins of Walsingham that are so vividly evoked in the poem. Saward *et al.* report that Philip visited Walsingham with the Queen. This would have been during his courtier days when the state of the ruins might have meant little to him. He would have had little sympathy for the severity of the Reformers in destroying the heritage of the Catholic Church, but nor did he take any vital interest in such matters at that time.

It was only later, with his new-found faith in the old religion and the one, true, Catholic Church, that he would have realised the enormity of the devastation, not just material but also, and principally, spiritual. The poem recalls the scene, acknowledging the 'blessings turned to blasphemies', for this was a shrine of the Blessed Virgin for whom Philip had conceived a great devotion. The poem expresses remorse and regret, especially with the events being barely a generation old. He saw how the desecration of the shrine was engraved in people's consciousness, whether in their satisfaction at the removal of vestiges of superstition or in a bitter grief over the division suffered in the country and at the lamentable repudiation of the old faith.

Philip appeals to the Virgin Mary to be his muse. Why? She is the Queen of Walsingham; it is her shrine. He speaks with pain of how the Mother of God was being insulted and rejected.

---

[6] Reprinted in Guiney, *Recusant Poets*, pp. 355–6.
[7] A copy of *The Wrackes of Walsingham* is in fact to be found bound together with *The Foure-fould Meditation* in the Bodleian Library, Rawlinson Poetry, 219 (Pollen and MacMahon, *Unpublished Documents*, p. 325).

She is the one affronted by the desecration of the shrine. And why was it raised to the ground? It was one of the four major pilgrimage destinations of Christendom. Henry VIII himself had made at least two pilgrimages to Walsingham. And yet the destroyers and iconoclasts of the Reformation treated it with sacrilegious contempt, even taking its precious statue of Our Lady to Chelsea to be burnt. The poem expresses the sadness that shows forth in Philip's other writings and poems at the reckless disregard for the truths of the traditional faith, and one senses the abject misery that the ruins of Walsingham now inspire in him.

> *Level level with the ground, the towers do lie,*
> *Which with their golden glittering tops*
> *Pierced once to the sky.*

Above all the poem affirms Philip's unselfish angst at the affront given to the Lord and his mother, 'Queene of Walsingham', by human pride and sinfulness. He expresses his grief at such desecration:

> *Then, thou Prince of Walsingham,*
> *Grant me to frame*
> *Bitter plaints to rue thy wrong,*
> *Bitter woe for thy name.*

The poem alludes to the 'silly sheep' (the archaic word *silly* meaning defenceless), that is the people belonging to the old faith who have been ostracised by the new regime and abandoned by so many of their shepherds, both bishops and clergy. The stately towers of the great church have been levelled to the ground. The towers of Walsingham were much more than a building, even more than a church. The poet takes them as a metaphor for what has happened to the Catholic faith under Henry VIII, Edward VI and Elizabeth. Once the pilgrimage destination of the nobility, Walsingham is now the haunt of owls and swine and, worse, of sin and of Satan:[8]

> *Sin is where Our Lady sat,*
> *Heaven turned is to hell,*

---

[8]   See the complete poem with its original spelling in Appendix A.

Satan sits where Our Lord did sway.
Walsingham Oh farewell!

Verses on the Passion The Passion of Christ was another
favoured theme in medieval devotion and poetry.[9] However,
this is not enough of an explanation as to why Philip was
drawn to compose his poem on the theme. It relates directly to
his fidelity to Christ whose readiness to undergo the ultimate
sacrifice for his sake he proclaims. Following his conversion,
and the change of life it brought about, it became important
for him to discover how to conceive of his time in the Tower
as something positive and willed for him by God. He began
to understand that it was a special grace, an opportunity to
return to the beginning, to recommence his spiritual journey
on a surer footing. He could not undo the past, but he could
make it a springboard for a future that was closer to the Lord.

All the Lord demanded of him was the sacrifice of 'a hum-
bled, contrite spirit' (Ps 51), so that he could recognise how
much he owed to the merciful God who had saved him by
his own sacrifice. The Passion of Christ is at the very centre of
Philip's prayer in the Tower. Christ's terrible sufferings allowed
him to forget his own afflictions. Instead, he could choose to
ask of the Lord that he might benefit from his torments by their
saving grace, each of them blessing him in different ways and
bringing him forgiveness, healing and holiness. He would not
be without all his afflictions for any prize, since they brought
him to the foot of the cross and rescued him for eternity.

As a sinner he knew he deserved to suffer and he would
rather it was in this life than the next. It was because of Christ's
Passion that he was able to do this, so each one of Christ's pains
won a reprieve for him, as they do for all repentant sinners.
He was able to meditate upon the crucifixion as a sure sign
of Christ's love and forgiveness. He loves us, no matter what
our condition as sinner or innocent, but his mercy is necessarily greater for the sinner because there is more to forgive.
For Philip, who longed to attend Holy Mass, but could not,
meditation on Christ's Passion was the next best way in which

---

9   Duffy, *Stripping the Altars*, pp. 234–8.

he could focus his devotion on the Lord's sacrifice and be associated with other sinners in coming to the throne of his mercy.

His poem is a deeply felt meditation on the redemptive value of Christ's sufferings, and a prayer for his grace and forgiveness:

> *O Christ my Lord which for my sins didst hang upon a tree,*
> *Grant that thy grace in me poor wretch may still ingrafted be.*

He invokes the Saviour's mercy through all the sufferings of his Passion, juxtaposing the pains of the crucifixion with the particular sins needing forgiveness:

> *Grant that thy naked hanging there may kill in me all pride,*
> *And care of wealth, since thou didst then in such poor state*
> *abide.*
>
> *Grant that those scorns and taunts which thou didst on the cross*
> *endure,*
> *May humble me and in my heart all patience still procure.*
>
> *Grant that thy praying for thy foes may plant within my breast,*
> *Such charity as from my heart I malice may detest.*

He concludes by reflecting on the blessings that are hoped for from the Resurrection and Ascension of Christ:

> *Grant that thy rising up from death may raise my thoughts from*
> *sin,*
> *Grant that thy parting from this earth from earth my heart may*
> *win.*
>
> *Grant Lord that thy ascending then may lift my mind to thee,*
> *That there my heart and joy may rest, though here in flesh I be.*[10]

There are two hymns appended to the first edition of Philip's Lanspergius translation at Lanherne Convent, but we have no guarantee of their provenance. They are entitled 'A hymne of the Life and Passion of Our Saviour' and 'A hymne wherein the Praises of all Creatures are offered up unto the Creator'.[11] The former has not proved possible to trace, but the latter is

---

[10] This short work deserves to be read in its entirety. See the poem in its original spelling in Appendix A.

[11] Pollen and MacMahon, *Unpublished Documents*, p. 328.

given in the *Arundel Hymnbook*, in a modernised text, as being by the Venerable Philip Howard, Earl of Arundel. The poem recalls the verses on heaven in the four-fold meditation. In it, Philip expresses his faith in simple words and without any shadow of fear. It is as if he senses his eternal destiny.

> *O Christ, the glorious Crown*
> *Of virgins that are pure,*
> *Who dost a love and thirst for Thee*
> *With-in their minds procure;*
> *Thou art the Spouse of those*
> *That chaste and humble be,*
> *The hope, the life, the only help*
> *Of such as trust in Thee.*
>
> *All charity of those*
> *Whose souls Thy love doth warm;*
> *All simple plainness of such minds*
> *As think no kind of harm;*
> *All sweet delights wherewith*
> *The patient hearts abound,*
> *Do blaze Thy Name, and with Thy praise*
> *They make the world resound.*

OTHER LETTERS BY PHILIP

Among letters Philip wrote from the Tower, we have passages quoted in the Arundel manuscript from those addressed to Robert Southwell on a number of occasions, and one to his wife when he felt that his death was approaching. In a letter to Robert, shortly after his trial and sentence, and while a prisoner in the Tower of London, he writes anticipating his execution and, in case he was not allowed to speak at the scaffold, he encloses a document for public distribution at his death setting out his affirmation of his innocence of treason and his readiness to die rather than forswear his Catholic faith (AM, pp. 99–102).

Though written quite early in his time in the Tower, this letter gives important clues as to Philip's state of mind, beliefs and commitments. There appear to be echoes of Campion's *Brag*, in that he confirms his absolute loyalty to the Catholic faith 'for which I am now ready to be executed'. In this, Philip shows himself to be an ardent witness for the truth, in his case even to the Queen to whom he had already addressed a letter protesting his innocence of any treason. At the same time the letter confirms him as a sign of contradiction in the society of which he was a member.

> Wherefore for the satisfaction of all men, and discharge of my conscience before God, I here protest before His Divine Majesty and all the Holy Court of Heaven, that I have committed no treason, and that the Catholick and Roman Faith which I hold, is the only cause (as far as I can any way imagine) why either I have been thus long imprisoned, or for which I am now ready to be executed. And I do most firmly, resolutely and unmoveably hold and believe this One, Holy, Catholick, and Apostolick Faith. And as I will die in the same so am I most ready at all times, if need be, to yield my life for defence thereof. And whatsoever the most sacred Council of Trent hath established touching faith and manners, I believe and hold. And whatsoever it hath condemned, I condemn in my soul, and renounce here under my hand, and abjure from the bottom of my heart.

He ends the letter wishing blessings upon Queen and country, but firm in his resolve to remain an obedient Catholic:

> beseeching Almighty God, the Father of mercies, and God of all consolation to grant peace unto His Church, charity and grace to mine enemies, salvation and felicity to the Queen, and realm, and to me as an untimely fruit (being born before my time) and the meanest of all His servants a constant perseverance in His Holy Faith and love of His Divine Majesty. Amen.
>   By me a most humble and obedient child of the Catholick Roman Church. Philipp Howard.[12]

On another occasion, but when he was expecting at any time to be executed, he wrote to Robert expressing his gratitude for the letters of comfort that the priest had addressed to him:

---

[12] See Appendix A for the complete text of the document.

My Dear and Rd. Father. This being the last time that
I think I shall ever send unto you, I should be very
ungrateful if, wanting all other means of expressing my
thankfulnesss, I should not now at least acknowledg it
in words; and as I must needs say, I could not be more
bound to any man, nor to any but one of your calling so
much; and all this in a time when such comforts were
most wellcome, and even to the benefit of that which
in all men is most pretious: so in heart, our Lord who
sees all secrets, sees my good will and thankfulness,
and I doubt not will reward you amongst all your
other worthy merits for these bestowed on me his most
unworthy servant; and in as much thankfullness and
good will as my heart can conceive, I remain yours till
the last moment. (AM, p. 134)

In a further letter to Robert he expresses himself with com-
mendable humility, 'What fault soever shall upon your own
knowledg find to be in me, and tell me of, I will always endeav-
our and desire to amend'. (AM, p. 137)

A letter to his wife Anticipating his death, he writes to his
wife, Anne, repenting of his neglect and his bad treatment of
her in the years when he was attending court:

Mine own good Wife. I must now in this world take
my last farewell of you, and as I know no person living
whom I have so much offended as yourself, so do I
account this opportunity of asking you forgiveness, as
a singular benefit of Almighty God, and I most humbly
and hartily beseech you even for His sake, and of your
charity to forgive me all whereinsoever I have offended
you, and the assurance thereof is a great contentment
to my soul at this present, and will be a greater I doubt
not when it is ready to depart out of my body; and I call
God to witness it is no smal grief unto me that I canot
make you recompence in this world for the wrongs I
have done you; for if it had pleased God to have granted
me longer life, I doubt not but you should have found
me as good a Husband to my poor ability by His grace,
as you have found me bad heretofore. (AM, p. 144)

These writings, both the poems and the letters, betoken someone who has come to terms with his fate and expects nothing to alter it. He has humbly absorbed the advice of Lanspergius and Robert Southwell, the two people who most brought him counsel. He has made his peace with the world, including as far as he is concerned with the Queen, but especially with his wife, and he stands ready for whatever is to follow. We are now ready to better understand his true sanctity and something of the journey he made from the secular to the spiritual world.

✣ 4 ✣

A Man of Faith

HIS FATEFUL DECISION

W E CAN SURELY FIND spiritual inspiration in St Philip, for he lived a far more radical change of heart than most people experience, and in more extreme circumstances. He did not flinch after his conversion. His moment of truth in the gallery of Arundel Castle must have brought him a powerful grace, as if he had been singled out, and this was the time when God's call came to him definitively. However, it was only when he began to consider reverting to the faith of his baptism that he adopted a style of life that could justly be called Christian. He began to exercise his responsibilities as a member of the House of Lords. He sought reconciliation with his neglected wife, and we learn of his deep regret for his treatment of her in the early days of their marriage (AM, pp. 144–5). He abandoned lavish living and he began to read about the faith. It was not long before he was reconciled to the Church, along with his brother William and following the example of his sister Margaret.

Philip was a very English saint. He never travelled abroad, though he could have done. He was a gentleman, a noble, of great intelligence, a Latin scholar in the medieval tradition with a decent learning acquired without studiousness. Despite the fact that he was known to have sown wild oats during his student days and in his life at Court, Philip was already admired for his intelligence, his generosity and the courtesy he showed to all. He could have lived a trouble-free existence with all doors open to him as the country's premier earl. Then suddenly all his assumptions were undermined. He felt the

51

necessity of being reconciled to the Catholic Church. His decision was betrayed on more than one occasion, and from then on it was disaster upon disaster.

His trial and imprisonment followed so quickly that it is impossible to say how much he might have changed if he had not been sent to the Tower. Dramatic change in his circumstances was forced upon him, and he lost control over his life, his freedom to come and go, and his enjoyment of plenty as one of the richest men in the realm. Above all, he suffered the disgrace of being treated as a criminal and deprived not only of his liberty but of virtually all contact with his family, friends and associates. He had also to endure the pain of injustice and of dealing with feelings of bitterness and resentment. As a person prominent in society he must have felt degraded at not knowing what was going on in the wider world of government and Church affairs. And, finally, he had no expectation of release and felt subject to the constant threat of execution.

In the ten remaining years of his life he would have thought constantly about death looming over him and the implication this had for how he was to live through hardship and tedium. He must have seen it as the opportunity to make his preparations for death, and his spiritual life can probably be best understood from this perspective. We might be tempted to discount the sufferings of those who have languished in prison for their faith as compared with those who went straight to execution. This is not to say that the scaffold represents an easier fate, but it may require less sustained courage than the daily treadmill of a long confinement. In any case, Philip faced both prospects as he remained under sentence of death for more than a quarter of his lifetime.

Since Philip had become reunited with his wife the joy of this relationship already contrasted greatly with his life as a courtier. In many ways his situation seemed to have turned out well. He was becoming convinced of the truth of the Catholic faith. There was a child in his family and another expected. Although he may have had a foreboding that all could not go on like this for ever, and that the crisis-point would come if he accepted to be reconciled with the Church, there was no way he could have anticipated the actual outcome. After his reconciliation he decided things could best be resolved by his leaving the country, but his plans began to collapse when his plan was betrayed, and he was apprehended at sea. Even then he did not see how grave his situation was. He expected to be reprimanded and then to be allowed to leave the country. Little did he realise that this was the end of his charmed life. He went to the Tower.

When, in the inscription he left in his cell, Philip spoke of his 'afflictions' we do well to remember how severe they were. He was locked up, indeed locked away, excluded from everything he had known as his own, his family, his social position and his possessions; and his very life was under threat. All this he had to endure confined to a cell which, as we learn from the Arundel manuscript, had little light and was filled with foul odours from nearby drains such as to cause him much discomfort and sickness. He had to resist the monotony of endless days, months and years and, worse, temptations to self-pity and possibly even to despair. Much of this treatment was common to other detainees in the Tower, but there were additional torments for Philip as a practising Catholic. The Mass and sacraments were denied him and yet he knew that these were the very essence of a life of faith.

The restrictions on his freedom were hard to bear. It was not merely the isolation and mistreatment that affected him; it was the emptiness, not having anyone to share his life with, no one to even talk to, no one with whom he could compare ideas and thoughts, and the absence of anyone on whom he could bestow affection or who could bring him words of reassurance. His most severe pain must have been to be separated from Anne, the wife with whom he had spent very few years since their reconciliation, and from his children, the youngest of whom he had never seen and would never see. Since he was not vowed to celibacy, this deprivation must have added greatly to his misery, with endless hours of pondering his fate. It was then that he most needed God's comfort, to save him from the despondency caused by the walls, the gloom, the cruelty of his jailers, the looming threat of worse to come and the end of hope in any human sense.

It is hard to imagine how Philip was able to survive such isolation without any human consolations. He resisted self-pity with great bravery. No doubt constantly tempted, at least in the early days, with the possibility of resolving his situation by agreeing to the royal demands, he instead forged another path, the path of faith, prayer and sanctity. Trustingly he turned to God. It was in his cause that he had ended up in the Tower. Could he not ask him for his help and consolation? How could he present his case to him? Would God hear his prayer? Light then began to dawn. Yes, God did hear him. He brought him such comfort that his prison became a sanctuary for him, a place where he could share in God's truth and goodness, a temple in which he could discover God and complete his conversion.

It was quite literally a miracle of grace that not only did he survive but he stayed awake, in that Gospel sense, and greatly advanced in sanctity. Through grace and his faith, he was able to accept his 'afflictions' and to offer them in union with those of Christ. In the Tower, the hope offered by Christ's resurrection was all he had to live for, and thus he made ten years of reparation by prayer and penance in virtual solitude. A touching story relates to the dog that Philip had as a companion and which appears beside his statue and in a stained-glass window in Arundel Cathedral. On one occasion, on being told that the dog had wandered into the cell in which Robert Southwell was being held, Philip, who must have had great affection for his dog, said that he loved the dog all the more for it.

What is the interpretive key to St Philip's spiritual or interior life that will help us to reach some understanding of his motivation and constancy as a believer, and even more than this to see in what way his experience can be spiritually meaningful for us today? Indeed, there is little point in examining his spiritual life unless we seek to learn from him in order to follow his example. He was certainly gifted by God with great faith but had virtually no one, apart from Robert Southwell for a few years, to whom he could turn for encouragement. He had known very few priests, and none of the martyrs directly, so we cannot look to his associates to help us understand him. How did he come to show such simple holiness? He was truly blessed with the gifts of the Holy Spirit, not just faith, but hope and peace, patience, a spirit of prayer and, quite evidently, freedom from doctrinal error.

Strangely though, the very severity of the rejection he suffered from the Queen and his peers strengthened his resolve to persevere in commitment to his faith. The Queen reacted to his reconciliation to the Church as if it were a personal affront. Everything was then interpreted to his disadvantage: his attempt to flee the country was an intimation of his disloyalty, not his fear of revenge; his first trial and the outrageous fine imposed convinced him of the regime's injustice; and this was followed by the second trial where, as was related above with reference to the cowardliness of Lord Derby, false evidence was introduced with complete unscrupulousness, rejected where it could not stick but sufficient to condemn him to death where it could not be absolutely refuted, such as the allegation that he had prayed for the success of the Armada.

All of this so impressed itself on Philip's mind that he could see no possible defence for the regime. It was confirming its own illegitimacy. There was nothing to be said for it in its state of corruption, and therefore he could not find any reconciliation but rather every justification for the contrarian course he had chosen. There is a certain doggedness about his spiritual path that contrasts, as was mentioned, with the joy-filled enthusiasm of so many of the priest-martyrs of the time. What emerges from the study of his writings is his sadness, and this has many dimensions. Apart from his sense of the displeasure of the Queen, there was the exile he suffered from his place in the realm, to add to all the other hardships and deprivations of his captivity. Not least, there was the realisation that all his protestations of innocence and goodwill counted for nothing.

Such an avalanche of misfortunes was a heavy burden for anyone to bear, and this perhaps explains the note of negative sentiments that runs through his writings, his lament for what might have been, his distress at the thought of sins deserving eternal punishment, his misery at the thought of Christ's Passion, though with the hope that these very sufferings would count for his redemption. He evidently began to ask himself what more he could do, how he could align himself with the martyrs who had given everything for their faith. He saw that the world had rejected him, and he could therefore reject the world with all its allurements. With what he had already lost it had nothing more to take from him that he valued, even his food. He committed himself to fasting even when it seemed potentially dangerous to his health or when he was ill. His writing was in part a protest or retaliation against the injustice of which he was being made the victim.

Despite all discouragement, what sustained Philip above all was his trust in God and in the Passion of Christ. He saw how Christ suffered on the Cross not just physically but spiritually as he saw people's infidelities and sins. Although Jesus came to call sinners not the just to repentance, he does this in sometimes surprising ways. Many people were devastated at the fate that befell Philip, a highly placed noble consigned to the dungeon, as they saw it. But the reality is that God chose a sure path to salvation for him. He had to move from horror at being cast into the Tower and being sentenced to death to trusting in God for everything. It was this conviction that made him a saint and martyr, and an unusual martyr too, because he was not actually killed, as far as we know, but left to die in such circumstances that the status of martyr was not denied him.

HIS SPIRITUAL PATH

He had barely three years between his first glimmer of faith at Edmund Campion's disputation and his being sent to the Tower. In that time, he had to take his bearings for the course he would follow and then begin to come to terms with what the Catholic faith was, and why he should adhere to it. He did not have the education of the missionary priests who had studied theology and spirituality for several years, and this on top of many years when they had been Catholic in spirit. He did not have anyone to whom he could turn for guidance in spiritual matters. He read works that had been recommended to him, but he was starting from ignorance of the faith. If he had had any idea of what awaited him he would have thought himself totally unprepared and he might have lost heart. There was certainly a grace that accompanied his reconciliation to the Church, and Fr Weston was a valuable resource for his guidance and advice at that stage. No doubt the opposition voiced by this priest to Philip's going abroad was in some measure due to his desire to help him further in his journey towards a more mature faith. He might well have listened to this counsel but for the fake reply he received to his letter to Cardinal Allen encouraging him to leave the country to join him. All this is to say that he was spiritually quite unprepared for his arrest and detention.

He was fortunate in his early days in the Tower to obtain the *Little Office of the Blessed Virgin*, the book on the Rosary and the work of Lanspergius. With little more than these resources he engaged in a kind of self-catechesis. Or rather we could say that God led him into Catholic faith by secret paths. He rapidly came to understand spiritual matters that were virtually new to him. He saw the sense of things that no one had explained. Not only did Church doctrine and spiritual teaching take shape for him but he also understood that it was possible that God had a purpose for him in prison, and this must have fortified him in the many examinations to which he was subjected by the Queen's councillors. Was this knowledge of the faith infused? He gives us no direct evidence of this, but at all events it was an accelerated spiritual and doctrinal formation that greatly strengthened him in the first years of his incarceration.

HIS ENCOUNTER WITH TRUTH

Philip was a saint who came to know the truth, that is, what is both objective and real, and ultimately the recognition of the transcendent being of the Blessed Trinity beyond which nothing can be conceived. Sanctity is the embrace and embracing of this truth. The martyrs encountered the real in God, known in Jesus Christ, and the truth not as a concept but from its source. Philip shows himself to be Christ-centred, turned away from the world. As St Paul says, 'These are a shadow of the things that were to come; the reality, however, is found in Christ' (Col 2: 17). He did not doubt this and was led deeper into truth the more he followed the path of a willing, living martyrdom. This fact was what made it impossible for the State authorities to appeal to Philip's private interest or even to plain reason that might have led him to compromise his faith. Philip knew the truth more by faith than by reason, if we are to judge by his writing. Again, as St Paul wrote, 'The righteous shall live by faith' (Rom 1: 17). Philip must have lived through a long dark night, but it is by faith that the righteous know God and come to live in his will. Faith aids their reason so that their righteousness is a reflection of the divine, an imitation of Christ, a sign of hope and expression of love. In fact, Philip represents a classic case of a conscience that would not permit itself to be violated but would moor itself to the truth.

His conversion was improbable. Perhaps if he had not attended Campion's disputation he might never have come to the encounter with truth that convicted him that day and led him eventually to abandon the worldly life at court to give witness to the old faith in a world that regarded him as near-royalty. But it was not a sudden Damascus Road experience. He hesitated, justifiably according to most of his contemporaries, since he would be giving up so many worldly advantages. He did not speak of his inmost thoughts, even to his wife who had already been reconciled to the Church. He simply surprised her by not opposing the step she had taken. However, there was a moment of decision for him while walking alone in the gallery of Arundel Castle. From that time the die was cast. He visited his brother, William, to encourage his conversion. He sought out Fr William Weston SJ who reconciled them both and offered 'such good directions for the amending and ordering of his life, as afterwards did greatly help and farther him therein' (AM, pp. 27–8).

We do not know if he had any mystical experience, but the change was total, and it seems certain that there was a powerful infusion of grace and enlightenment. The process may have been slow, but it was sure. He found the truth, and from then until his death he was faithful to it. He believed in the one, true Church and its sacraments. He developed a life of fervent prayer and came to a strong devotion to the Blessed Virgin. We can marvel at the thoroughness of this conversion. It was a veritable return to innocence, all the more remarkable for being such a different path from that followed by a typical Elizabethan courtier. And another contrast with the conversion of St Paul: while the great apostle was commissioned to go out and preach the gospel to the whole world, St Philip was sent into the desert of the Tower of London, isolated from the world but as a powerful though nearly silent witness to the gospel for the remaining years of his life.

His experience of being detained, however, was paradoxically spiritual. The world becomes a prison for the unbeliever, but he cannot see its walls until he glimpses the spiritual universe beyond. Philip was imprisoned in the world, but liberated in his cell, because he recognised the truth that set him free. Although alone, confined, sick, yet persevering in his service to God through his prayer and work, Philip found a deeper faith and a fuller truth in his life of solitude and prayer (AM, p. 70). His commitment was such that not even for the joy of seeing his wife and children was he ready to act against his conscience by attending a Protestant service.

It seems that Philip never doubted, and thus was led deeper into truth and goodness. He rejected the transient honours and satisfactions of his noble heritage, the court, the pursuit of riches and personal favours, freedom of affections and lifestyle. He accepted poverty, pain, loneliness and sickness as his way of the cross. In this he never wavered. How could Philip return to his former life and be reconciled to the regime that had shown him such injustice, when all he had come to know of the Catholic Church was honourable, merciful and worthy of belief? We can only marvel at the strength of faith he showed in standing up to the public obloquy he continually suffered from public officials. The unjust attitude of the regime to him was sustained even in the sermon preached at his funeral.

> Mr. Lieutenaunt being asked whether he had any direction of any service to be used at the burial, and whether he dyed with any relenting in his former courses & unto both he aunswering, No: The minister began thus.

We are not come to honour this man's religion. We publicly profess, and here openly protest otherwyse to be saved: nor to honour his offence: the law hath iudged him, and we leave him to the lord, he is gone to his place . . . Thus God hath layd this man's honour in the dust . . . so we committ his bodye to the earth, geving God harty thanks that he hath delyvered us of so great a feare . . . Lord, shield our soveraigne, exalt thyne annoynted, with thy hand assist, & thy right arme defend her, never let her foes prevayl against her, nor the chylde of wickednes bringe her to destruction: Banish from her court all her privye enemyes, & kepe her evermore from dissembling frends.[1]

[1]   Pollen and MacMahon, *Unpublished Documents*, pp. 333–5.

✤ 5 ✤

A Man of Prayer

HIS LIFE OF PRAYER

W E KNOW THAT PHILIP gave himself to a life of prayer, study and spiritual writing, thus making the most, according to his convictions, of his extended imprisonment. Being under sentence of death, he continually expresses his readiness to die and his determination to stay faithful to the Catholic Church. In a letter to Fr Southwell, soon after his condemnation, he writes,

> It is my dayly Prayer I call our Lord to witness, that I may continue constant in the profession of His Catholick Faith to the end, and in the end; come life or death or whatever else. And He knows, who knows the secrets of all hearts, that I am fully resolved to endure any death, rather than willingly yield to anything offensive to His Divine Majesty in the least respect, or to give just cause of scandal to the meanest Catholick. (AM, pp. 147–8)

From the Arundel manuscript we learn (pp. 105–11) that his prayer life, with very few opportunities to hear Mass and receive Holy Communion, was based on the Divine Office (p. 105), devotion to the Mother of God through praying the *Little Office of Our Lady* (p. 108) and the Rosary (p. 120), and we are told that he spent long hours in personal prayer (p. 105). We can imagine his prayer, Christ-centred, offering his afflictions, praying for forgiveness for his past sins, trusting in God's promises, and living in humble obedience to God's will. It is likely that he would have known by heart the Magnificat, the Blessed Virgin's canticle of hope and trust, which could have seemed to him to offer solace in his own situation, 'He has mercy on those who fear him in every generation'.

He embraced the life of a contemplative, a religious in the lay state. Unable to hear Mass or to receive the other sacraments for years, he took up the Rosary, a contemplative prayer; it was his sacrament, an outward sign of the inward grace of peace and love, a veritable symbol of Catholic fortitude in his times. Although we cannot know how Philip would have prayed it, one who faithfully prays the Rosary is constantly aware of the meaning that the lives of Jesus and Mary holds for the believer. Inspired by its joyful, sorrowful and glorious mysteries, Philip would have meditated on the Incarnation and the life of the Holy Family, the Passion of Christ and his forgiveness of sins, and the glories of heaven with the new life promised to believers in the company of the Blessed Trinity and Mary, Queen of Mothers.

As we saw in Philip's poem on the Passion, he extols the loving sacrifice of Christ in his Crucifixion and all the saving graces that it has brought to us. We can imagine walking through Christ's passion with Philip, following the Way of the Cross. How might the fourteen stations have brought him insight and comfort in his own situation?

1. Jesus judged: Philip, you too accepted to be falsely condemned.
2. The Cross: you took the cross offered to you, in love of Christ and in penance for sin.
3. The first fall: you prayed not to fall into sin now that the self-indulgence of the past was rejected.
4. Jesus meets Mary: you shared Mary's sorrow by your compassion.
5. Simon of Cyrene: you helped Jesus to carry the Cross by uniting your sufferings with his.
6. Veronica wipes the face of Jesus: you conceived an image of the Passion of Jesus and sought to comfort him.
7. The second fall: you hoped by God's mercy to be saved from eternal punishment, and even from 'the purging fire'.
8. The women of Jerusalem: you desired to express your contrition deeply by your penitential life.

9. The third fall: you carried your cross with perseverance, aided by God's grace and mercy.
10. Jesus is stripped: you too were stripped, of lands, wealth and family.
11. Jesus is nailed to the Cross: you were forced to mortify all your earthly passions and desires.
12. Jesus dies: you hoped to die with Jesus' name on your lips.
13. Mary receives the body of Jesus: you sought to comfort Our Lady by your commiseration in her grief.
14. Jesus is laid in the tomb: your body was worn out, but in your spirit you had a secure hope of resurrection.

We should not be under any illusions about Philip's life of prayer; it was exceptional and only possible in God's strength. He began each day wondering if it was to be his last. He gave himself to prayer when there seemed to be no response and no let-up in his hardships. He disciplined himself to continue with his writing, not knowing if it would survive or ever benefit anyone else. He had to maintain his self-respect when he was being treated with contempt by his jailers. Without any real hope of release, he had to fight off any temptation to despair. We also learn that, from 1588, he fasted strictly on Mondays, Wednesdays and Fridays until a short time before his death, as was reported to the writer of the Arundel manuscript by one of Philip's servants who was allowed to attend him (AM, pp. 107–8). Philip's holiness must have come out of much prayer. The details that the Arundel manuscript gives us are most likely accurate since they come from a person experienced in the spiritual life who strove to ground all the other information he gives us about Philip on what he learnt from people in direct, or privileged indirect contact with him during his years in the Tower.

HIS CONTRITION AND HIS LOVE FOR THE LORD

From his *Foure-fould Meditation* poem we have seen how Philip views the souls of sinners especially in need of God's mercy. Here we sense the depth of his sorrow for his own sins and for the evils of society. Philip knew a world riven with scandal, compromise, corruption and lethargy, at court, amongst ecclesiastics and even amongst faithless Catholics. This must have both saddened him and heightened his love for the forsaken Christ. Indeed, his own judgement and condemnation made him a fellow-sufferer with the Lord. It is relevant to ask how Philip conceived his love for Christ. We need to learn love, yet Philip had had no loving mother to raise him, a father who was never close, and otherwise only relatives, a tutor, and some well-disposed adult figures. Nor did he get married for love, since it was all arranged for him. He cannot have found love at court. The Queen was to be respected, and even feared, but not loved, and he was in competition with other courtiers for favour. And there may have been other kinds of love, which were not love at all, before his finally finding a new tenderness for his wife, Anne, who had shown him true affection and was solicitous in giving him what care she could when he was sent to the Tower.

Everything of significance began with his reconciliation to the Church. It was love of God and the Virgin Mary that awakened him to true love, and this extended itself to Anne, and then to others, his benefactors, Robert, and no doubt we should not forget the faithful dog! So, spiritually he was requited, but in human terms he was very restricted. There is much to learn from St Philip's own life of humility, repentance, piety, perseverance, integrity and generosity as an evident example to Christians of any era. He becomes an outsider to society but perseveres in commitment to God in conscience to the point of giving up seeing his wife and children to remain faithful. What we can say is that in a certain sense Philip's life was decided for him once he had made his reconciliation. Although it ran counter to his previous life, he accepted it in obedience and spent the prime of his adult life dedicated with the utmost faith and perseverance to God. He knew that if he shared Christ's sufferings he would share his glory, so that he could actually be grateful to God and praise him for the bitter pains he had to undergo.

A Man of Prayer

HIS BELIEF IN GOD'S MERCY

We learn of the great confidence Philip had in the mercy and goodness of Almighty God from a letter he wrote to a friend:

> I assure you I prepare myself as much as my weakness and frailty will permitt, and I had rather perform more, than come short of that I promise, especially wherein my frailty and unworthiness and infinit sins may justly make me doubt of the performance. But I know God's mercy is above all and I am sure He will never suffer me to be tempted above my strengt; and upon this I build with all assurance and comfort. (AM, p. 155)

Imprisonment had revealed to Philip the nothingness of worldly life, the very life in which he had engaged so willingly. He came to see that his confinement was in fact a privilege, a time when he could make reparation for sin, his own and that of others, especially of those who had treated him with injustice and cruelty. He would surely have liked to have been able to have the help of a priest to discern the way to deal with many spiritual issues that arose for him, yet he had all the help he really needed from a merciful God. He knew he was forgiven and that there was no obstacle between God and himself that grace could not remove.

He made a willing offering of his life, his adversities, his goods and his heart since he believed in divine mercy. He understood that the counterpart of God's mercy was forgiveness, a virtue that he not only saw in God but to which he himself aspired with no edge of resentment or bitterness, but rather with a humble desire for reconciliation, including with the Queen who remained obdurate in her attitude towards him. He learned to behave towards others as he would have wanted them to behave towards him. The fact that they often did not reciprocate was a matter of indifference to him once he had set his sights on serving Jesus Christ.

His open secret was to seek to be Christ-like. In this he knew would be found the solution to all the ills of society, if each person decided for God and persevered to the end, never abandoning him and never rejecting their neighbour. One of Philip's characteristics brought out by the Arundel manuscript was his gratitude for all kindnesses (AM, p. 133). Further, we learn that he was a generous soul given to numerous almsdeeds (AM, p. 131). From the Tower he made provision, insofar as he was able, for the payment of all his debts and for the bequest of two of his houses to religious orders:

> I pray you let my Son know when he comes to any years of discretion, that I was fully resolved to make Howard-house and Norwich house religious houses, and to restore all religious lands (if I had lived to see a Catholick time) and desire him for the love of God and on my blessing to do the like (for so God will prosper him) except he shall be otherwise advised by such as I submit my self to their judgment. (p. 158)

He also intended to found a chantry:

> I have appointed 2500 pounds for the building of a Chantry, which I wish my Son to do, if ever he be able, or those that have dealing in my lands before he come of age, if the time serve, and the lands be restored. (p. 159)

We can imagine that from the spiritual counsel in Robert Southwell's letters of comfort he derived some of his strength to endure his prison. By Lanspergius' *Epistle of Jesus Christ* he may have been helped to be reconciled to his fate without self-pity through an invincible trust in God's mercy. He certainly found greater peace with the teaching that by his sufferings he was building-up treasure in heaven.

HIS SHARING IN THE WITNESS OF THE MARTYRS OF HIS TIME

Philip was not physically tortured nor put to death by violent means. His was a psychological and spiritual pain, more like the agony in the garden than the Crucifixion, or perhaps the hidden and mystical wounds of the Blessed Virgin Mary that earned her the title of Queen of Martyrs. Remarkably, Philip voluntarily added to his pains through his self-denial and by praying in a kneeling position that blackened and scarred his knees (AM, p. 109). In accepting his detention without complaint and the cruel treatment he received as his preparation for death, Philip offers us a model of holiness. It was surely one of the pillars of his sanctity that he was obedient without resentment to what he saw as God's will.

He understood that he could be a witness to others. Many people knew of his fate and were commiserating. He saw that he was able to influence the thoughts of many just by being the obstinate witness for God that he was. So many could see the injustices and cruelties of the Elizabethan regime, and even if they did nothing to protest there was a revolt in their hearts which helped sustain the recusant people and its martyrs. Even if he was not directly aware of this he trusted that it was so, especially when he had it affirmed by the pen of Robert Southwell.

What made his slow martyrdom worthwhile? He knew he could have his liberty restored if he was willing to compromise by turning away from the Catholic faith. However, in the face of oppression and injustice he showed himself faithful. There is abundant evidence of his growing holiness. Of his spiritual qualities the evidence lies in many of his letters. Of his constancy in adversity we can judge from a letter he wrote to Robert Southwell 'For all Crosses touching worldly matters, I thank God they trouble me not much, and much the less for your singular good Counsel, which I beseech our Lord I may often remember' (AM, p. 152). He lived in an invisible Catholic community of love and witness: Gregory Martin, his childhood tutor, Edmund Campion, Robert Southwell, William Weston, his family, and many other fellow martyrs. He desired holiness for all, but he had to abandon any active apostolate and just be for God.

He made a sacrifice of his life in the hope of glory. He would not have been able to endure so much were it not for divine grace. Where did he source this spirit of faith apart from the depth of his prayers? There is no doubt that he emphasises the dark side rather than the exultation of the spiritual life. Philip was living a torment, holding on by prayer to his faith as a lifeline, while denied the Mass and sacraments. However, he expected and indeed wished for a martyr's death. His servants attested that one day he pointed his finger towards Tower Hill, and told them that had it been God's will, he desired much more to have died for his faith upon that hill than in his bed, as now it seemed likely he would do (AM, p. 157).

HIS ACCEPTANCE OF DEATH

In a letter to his wife, Anne, when near to death, he writes of his readiness to die, intimating the possibility of his being killed unlawfully:

> I beseech you for the love of God to comfort yourself whatever shall happen, and to be best pleased with that, which shall please God best and be His will to send. For mine own part I find by more arguments than those I understand from you, that there is some intent (as they think who work it) to do me no good, but indeed to do me the most good of all: but I am, I thank God, and doubt not but I shall be by his grace, ready to endure the worst which flesh and blood can do against me. (AM, p. 153)

Philip accepted his coming death. It even appears that he had foreknowledge of the day of his death and was preparing for it particularly during the final week of his life. He expressed no regrets for his life other than his mistreatment of Anne, even though he recognised his many failings and weaknesses. He trusted that he was going to meet his Saviour. He had followed as best he could the teachings and commandments of the faith and had lived up to the testament of the inscription he left in his cell. He made the sacrifice of acceptance of God's will to the uttermost. He valued the world but little except for the blessing of his wife, as he told her in his last communication:

> I call God to witness that if it were not in respect of you (albeit I lived) every body should well see, if I were not utterly kept from it against my will, that I esteem as little of the world, as she by her usage has seemed to esteem of me, and that I despised her as much as she did me.

In the same letter he spoke of his desire, if Anne predeceased him and he was not executed, to enter religious life.

> If you should not do well, I would (if the Queen took me
> not away by a violent death), voluntarily sequester my
> self from this sea of misery, or els want of my will. (AM,
> pp. 159–60)

In other words, he had become familiar with the contemplative
life and was resolved to prolong it if he survived the Tower.
Here we have the evidence of Philip's underlying motivation
in his life. He was fully committed to God and to the faith. He
had been inspired by the Scriptures and spiritual writings,
the holiness of significant people in his life such as Edmund
Campion, Robert Southwell, Cardinal Allen, Lanspergius, the
many martyrs of whom Eusebius wrote, and perhaps not least
by his wife, Anne. He must in the end have seen his incarceration as a grace from God, the opportunity to reach sanctity and
to crown his earthly life as a pilgrimage towards eternal life.

The Queen had made a kind of promise that before his death
his wife and children could come to see him. When Philip was
expecting soon to die he appealed to Elizabeth. She replied
verbally through the Tower lieutenant that if he attended the
Protestant service he would see his wife and children and be
restored to his former status. Philip, however, is reported to
have said that 'he could not accept her Majesty's offers upon
that condition; adding withall that he was sorry he had but
one life to lose for that cause' (AM, p. 115).

After this Philip became more ill to the point that he ceased
reading the Divine Office and only prayed the Rosary, and this
until his death. One of his last conversations, as reported in the
Arundel manuscript, was with Sir Michael Blount, the Tower
lieutenant who came to ask him for his forgiveness for treating
him so badly. Philip forgave him but in an extraordinary way,
warning him not to mistreat other prisoners who were already
greatly distressed, since 'God, who with his finger turneth the
unstable wheel of this variable world, can in the revolution
of a few days, bring you to be a prisoner also, and to be kept
in the same place where now thou keep others.' And this is
what subsequently happened within a few weeks of Philip's
death, when the Lieutenant fell into disgrace and was himself
imprisoned in the Tower (AM, p. 118–19).

The Arundel manuscript gives a detailed account of Philip's last day, though we do not know its sources. He is believed to have asked for the assistance of Fr Weston at his death, but neither he nor any other priest was permitted to attend him (AM, p. 114). We are told that he spent the day praying the Rosary and some prayers he knew by heart, especially invoking the names of Jesus and Mary. He knew he was dying. When the time came,

> lying on his back, his eyes firmly fixt towards heaven and his long lean and consumed arms out of the bed, his hand upon his breast, laid in cross one upon the other, about twelve o'clock at noon, in which hour he was also born into this world, arraign'd, condemned and adjudg'd unto death, upon Sunday the 19th of October 1595 (after almost 11 years Imprisonment in the Tower) in a most sweet manner without any sign of grief or groan, only turning his head a little aside, as one falling into a pleasing sleep, he surrender'd his happy soul into the hands of Almighty God, who to his so great glory had created it. (AM, p. 121)

His will, dated 12 June 1588, opens with the following striking words:

> In nomine patris et filii et spiritus Sancti, Amen. I, Philippe Erle of Arundell, being a member of the trewe, auncient Catholique and Apostolick Church &c. of sound and perfect memorie do make my last will and testament as followeth. I bequeath my soule into the handes of the most gloriouse and inseparable Trinitie, one trewe Almightie and everlasting God, and my bodie to be buried in such place as my executors shall appoint.[1]

CONCLUSION

What can we conclude about the interior life of St Philip? He was truly blameless from the time of his conversion, not just for the crimes of which he was accused but in his prayer life

---

[1]   Pollen and MacMahon, *Unpublished Documents*, p. 370.

and his human relationships. He proved himself completely loyal to Jesus, to his spiritual mother, Mary, and to the Catholic faith, practising the Gospel injunction to 'stand ready' since he did not know the day or the hour when he might be put to death. He separated himself spiritually from the world from which he had been physically isolated, accepting that he would never be freed. He expressed his own contrition in his meditative poem on the four last things. He offered up his enforced celibacy, when he could have returned to his wife by apostasising. He never condemned his enemies, those who had unjustly condemned him. He showed his love for others by his gentleness, humility and generosity. He had a special apostolate and destiny by God's grace. In sum, he was possessed by the truth for which he yearned. He was single-minded in his lack of compromise. God was his ultimate reality. He expressed his dependence on God by constant prayer until the time when he could live that reliance fully in heaven. Now that he is at peace in glory, he can forget the sufferings he was obliged to endure.

✢ 6 ✢

Testimonies to Philip's Sanctity

N UMBERED AMONG THE FORTY MARTYRS of England and
Wales, St Philip was canonised not only because he
was considered a martyr by his being left to die in
captivity but because of his sanctity. One way we can know that
we are in contact with the truth is by contemplating examples
of heroic faith, unflinching endurance and holiness such as St
Philip's. He came to see God as the fundamental reality. This
insight, demanding humility to the point of tears, makes sense
out of his contemplative life as an openness to what was real.
That is, we may live our lives on this earth as effectively as we
are able, but what use will our efforts be unless we accept the
very first premise, as lived by St Philip, that we are created
by and for God, and that this truth is conveyed to us by the
Incarnation, Passion and Resurrection of Jesus Christ?

No doubt the most important testimonies to Philip's sanctity are the decisions of the Congregation for the Causes of
Saints in favour of his beatification (1929) and his canonisation
(1970), and the Mass readings assigned by the Church for his
feast-day. The information provided by the postulators to the
Congregation in Rome is heavily reliant upon the Arundel
manuscript. The importance of this is that the Congregation
must have been willing to place enough trust in this source
to support its decision in favour of the beatification. What,
however, is particularly interesting is that the commission that
looked at the evidence was not unanimous in its recommen-
dation. Two of the nine commissioners were unfavourable.
The issue was whether Philip could be called a martyr, which
would have gained his beatification instant approval. The
commissioners were agreed on how significant his case was,

how eminent a person he was amongst English Catholics, and even that his hardship readily undergone had made reparation for his misspent youth. Moreover, it was acknowledged that his punishment was solely due to the fact that he was a Catholic. The problem for the commissioners lay in whether he actually died for the faith. His condemnation to death had in effect been commuted to imprisonment by the Queen since she did not sign his death warrant. His demise was not 'from hardships continued to death' (*ex aerumnis ad mortem continuatis*). The hesitations continued, 'There is no actual shedding of blood; he was not fettered or tortured in prison, nor killed by squalor or want of food' (*Verum effusio sanguinis deest; ipse autem non vinctus, non cruciatus in carcere fuit, nec squalore aut inedia peremptus*).[1] However, the argument that his sufferings led to his death carried the day.

The readings designated for the Mass of St Philip for his feast-day on 19 October in the diocese of Arundel and Brighton, of which he is co-patron, capture perfectly the nature of his sanctity and the way he set out to practise his faith. Thus, the first reading (Wisdom 3: 1–9), which could have been one of the scriptural sources for Philip's inscription in his cell, begins:

> The souls of the virtuous are in the hands of God; no torment shall ever touch them . . . If they experienced punishment as men see it, their hope was rich with immortality; slight was their affliction, great will their blessings be.

The responsorial psalm (Ps 30) expresses the soul's reliance on God alone: 'My life is in your hands, deliver me from the hands of those who hate me'. The second reading (2 Cor 4: 7–15) also expresses the faith that characterised St Philip:

> We are only the earthenware jars that hold this treasure, to make it clear that such an overwhelming power comes from God and not from us . . . We are consigned to our death every day, for the sake of Jesus, so that in our mortal flesh the life of Jesus, too, may be openly shown.

---

1   *Relazione del promotore generale della fede, intorno ai martiri d'Inghilterra*, 27 October 1929 (Jesuits in Britain Archives).

There follows the Gospel reading (Mt 10: 18–22) which almost word for word sums up the latter years of St Philip's life:

> You will be dragged before governors and kings for my sake, to bear witness before them and the pagans ... You will be hated by all men on account of my name; but the man who stands firm to the end will be saved.

There are also several near-contemporary testimonies that need to be considered. First, there is the evidence we have through the chronicler of Philip's and his wife's lives, the anonymous Jesuit who heard from Countess Anne details of how Philip lived his prison years. This is the work written after his death, and to which we have continually had recourse in this account of St Philip's life, several chapters of which are devoted to recounting his moral and spiritual virtues. We can also be enlightened by the witness of St Robert Southwell who corresponded with Philip during the last few years of his life and thought him deserving of his lengthy letters of comfort. Although the two men never met, Robert knew Philip indirectly through his role as chaplain to Countess Anne and through his correspondence with him, and evidently felt sure of his judgement of Philip's virtue, as he makes clear in his *Epistle of Comfort* and in his poem, *I Dye without Desert*.[2]

> *A gracious plant for fruit, for leaf, for flower,*
> *A peerless gem for virtue, proof and price,*
> *A noble peer for prowess, wit and power,*
> *A friend to truth, a foe I was to vice.*
> *And lo, alas! now innocent I die,*
> *A case that might even make the stones to cry.*

Even if those who assume that this poem refers to Philip are incorrect, there is still the direct and detailed testimony of Robert Southwell that is contained in the letter he wrote to Philip that was briefly cited above, but which is of such significance as to be worth further quoting:

> For your cause—by whatever name it may be disfigured, by what ever colour deformed in the eyes of men—is

---

[2] See the full text of the poem in its original spelling in Appendix A.

religion. The form of the accusation itself speaks this; all the more prudent and sedate think it; all the rest of the charges alleged prove it. Proceed with the patience and equanimity you have hitherto done, and whatever be said by the envious, the Psalmist's words will be true in this your calamity, *In memoria aeterna erit Justus, ab auditione mala non timebit!* (The just man shall be in everlasting remembrance; he shall not fear bad news!)

Many sigh for thee; the tears of many flow for thee; never was dying man more justly lamented. Men everywhere predict that your constancy in death, your humility in suffering will profit the Church of God far more than the labours of a long life, so indignant are all men with this iniquitous sentence. Martyrdom confers the highest honour on any man: to you it will bring a double palm, for you. will be able to say with the psalmist, *Praestitisti decori meo virtutem* (You have given strength to my beauty), since you have crowned nobility with the cross of Christ. If thou hast sinned, no sacrament more powerful than such a death, no satisfaction more valid. If you are well-deserving (as indeed I think) no crown more excellent, no laurel more glorious than martyrdom.

Let therefore neither fury nor fiction nor the sword, nor glory of splendid attire, nor bribes, nor entreaties, nor any other violence seduce thee from the charity of Christ. Thou wast born that thou mightest be of God. That thou livest is from God. Thou encounterest this death for God. That death will confirm the vacillating, will render the strong yet stronger still. Friends applaud, strangers are astonished, adversaries are confounded, whilst you beget for yourself in both worlds an eternal name. A happy beginning gains a more happy conclusion for him, whom hitherto neither a long imprisonment nor the sentence of death, nor the hope of pardon, nor deceitful promises soften. The cause is God's, the conflict short, the reward eternal.

Lastly to treat of the affairs of your soul. I would not that you afflict yourself too much by fasting, prayers and penitential works, in order that you may be the stronger for the last combat. Your desire of confessing, the means being now precluded, and the contrition of a humble heart, expressed by shedding your blood in this cause, will be as full a remission of sins and of all punishment due for them, as in baptism, so great is the prerogative of martyrdom. I desire you the happiest issue of the conflict begun. Let us hope by the help of God to see each other hereafter in glory. Farewell.[3]

A famed contemporary of Philip, the Flemish theologian Cornelius a Lapide SJ, was one of those who praised his spiritual zeal in almost extravagant terms. On reflection, it speaks volumes for the widespread consternation caused by the Earl's judicial condemnation that, in his lengthy and scholarly commentaries on the New Testament, a continental theologian should have chosen Philip to illustrate the verse in Hebrews (10:34) 'For you not only shared the sufferings of those who were in prison, but you happily accepted being stripped of your belongings', saying:

> he died in durance a glorious confessor, yea, a martyr. He was the chief earl of England, and of a most noble family, and wonderful it is how much he lost, and with what quietness of mind he endured all adversities. Whilst he was a prisoner he was not only of example, but a singular comfort for all Catholics. No one ever heard him complain either of the loss of his goods or of the incommodities of the prison, or the being bereaved of his liberty; and such as heard complain or understood to be aggrieved, he endeavoured by his words and courteous usage to comfort, strengthen and confirm. His delight was in nothing but God, and the contemplation of heavenly things. Much of the money which the Queen did allow him for his maintenance (for to every prisoner in the Tower something is assigned, more or less according to each man's degree) he gave unto the poor, contenting himself with a spare and slender diet. Many other things this most noble Earl said, did and suffered, which equal if not exceed the deeds of the ancient worthies of the primitive Church and therefore are most worthy to be eternalised. (AM, pp. 162–4)

---

3   Published by H. More, *Historia Provinciae Anglicanae* (1660), p. 186.

In concluding his biography of Philip, the author of the Arundel manuscript gives his own verdict which, not insignificantly, is concluded with a resounding 'Amen'.

> That which this author saith of the Earl that he was a glorious Confessor of the Catholick faith, yea a Martyr, is the general persuasion of all learned Catholick men, both of our own and other nations. As such therefore we all ought to esteem him, and may with just reason commend our selves to his holy Prayers and Intercession, that thereby we may obtain so much grace of Almighty God, that here we may imitate his excellent virtues, and in heaven enjoy his happy company for all eternity. Amen. (AM, p. 164)

Here we see suggested a confirmation of Philip's sanctity, from 'our own and other nations', that might well be taken as commending him to our own age. For his perseverance in his faith, St Philip, like all those who suffered grievously or who gave their lives for the faith in those times, is an enduring sign for Catholic believers.

The Enduring Relevance
of St Philip's Witness

I T WOULD BE TO TAKE A LIMITED VIEW of a saint's or martyr's life if we did not reflect upon its relevance to the wider world. We can look at these lives in the light of eternity, for they are lived in that sense and only take on their full meaning when these saints take their place in heaven. Here I want to consider the implications of St Philip's life and experience for the world today, though it is not for their expertise in resolving our problems that we turn to the martyrs but to be inspired by their faith and holiness, and to seek their prayers of intercession. Indeed, there would be little point in our reflecting on a martyr's life if we did not ask for his or her prayers. In other words, what relevance does St Philip's interior life have for people today when they, like Philip, are pressured to conform morally, spiritually and practically to prevailing currents of official thought and culture?

Philip's life is to be understood in the circumstances of the early Reformation, the age of the destruction of the fabric of Catholic life and of untold harm done to souls, to culture and to the entire realm. It is this context that gives meaning to his life and martyrdom. For a panoramic view of the life-and-death existence of Catholics in England during Philip's years as an active Catholic there is probably no better text than Caraman's *Henry Garnet*.[1] However, it is notable that this work scarcely mentions Philip, other than to report his sentencing and his death, in spite of the fact that considerable attention is given

---

[1]   Caraman, *Henry Garnet*.

to the prison life and hardships of a large number of other people, many of them clergy, and especially Jesuits. It is hard to account for this neglect, when so many at the time were shocked at Philip's condemnation, and thus there is all the more reason now to recall what he endured to preserve the depth and constancy of his faithful witness and to consider its relevance for our contemporary world.

There is no doubt that the saints and martyrs offer us insight and help in facing perennial concerns. This is not to say that specific questions linked to current economic or cultural matters can be directly addressed by reflecting upon St Philip's life, but there are certainly principles that can be derived from or which are exemplified in his experience of his world that can be applied to ongoing ethical and spiritual concerns and action. Indeed, the Gospel admonishes us that we should read the 'signs of the times' and be 'wise as serpents' concerning the errors of our times in faith and morals. Faithful Christian believers are becoming increasingly concerned by the state of the world, its amorality, its rebellion, its pride and lack of openness to God's words of truth. Western society is ever more prone to denying its historical roots in Christianity. There is no longer a clear basis for ethics or morality other than the passing fads of socially approved values and the groundless belief in constant progress towards more valid ethical positions.[2]

We can certainly say that these issues are not being clarified despite much polemic and debate. People can be so busy with daily life, work, social intercourse, relationships, and merely looking after themselves, that their minds are overwhelmed. How can most people find the time or even the inclination to reflect on God, the four last things, or even on whether their lives are good and purposeful? Surely this can be the only explanation why so many do not seem to consider the possibility of God's existence, or the meaning it could give to their lives and destinies. We could almost be driven to envy of a man who was afforded a decade of seclusion to meditate

---

[2] For his portrayal and analysis of what he called the 'dictatorship of relativism', see Pope Benedict XVI, *Values in a Time of Upheaval* (San Francisco: Ignatius Press, 2006).

on these matters. At the very least we can reflect on how we might invite St Philip's intercession in many situations of need in which we find ourselves today.

We live in a time of secular materialistic thinking typified by consumerism, advertising and the hypnotic character of the mass media and social media, along with their concomitant fake news and false prophets. There is a loss of a sense of truth. The falsehoods of contemporary society are legion, in moral relativism, religious indifference and scientism. Can anything be said from the perspective of Elizabethan society about such issues? Philip himself suffered directly from false accusations of treason and from lies taken as evidence at his trial and, even more, he was deprived of title and property on account of his religious beliefs.

The new religion imposed on English society in the sixteenth century failed to inherit the piety of the people. In place of the old religion of popular devotion came one of enforcement, like the virtually mandatory secular values of our time that make people afraid, or even legally forbidden, to speak of what they truly think, believe or desire. In Philip's time, Catholics were outlawed by the ordinances of a state religion, while today Catholic faith is being gradually proscribed by secular society's new laws and principles. The fact is that there is not so much difference as might at first be thought between Philip's society and our own. Because of his sacrifice of his marriage and children, and his commitment to reconciliation with his wife, St Philip has been named as the patron of separated spouses. This is a vital cause in our day when the very institution of marriage is threatened by egoism and a false idea of freedom. Philip is a saint who willingly surrendered the worldly inducements of freedom and even accepted the cruel sundering of his links with his wife and children. The same courage is required by those of Christian conviction to stand up to the strictures and laws of contemporary culture and society so as to proclaim the primacy of eternal truths, and so St Philip can surely be relied upon to give us the help of his prayers.

Contemporary culture and Protestantism have conserved the tenets of the Reformation in their rejection of the authority of the Church vested in the Bishop of Rome, of the sacraments and their efficacy, of the special role of Mary and the saints, of the so-called *non-biblical* doctrine of Purgatory and, for many, in espousing a fundamentalist reliance upon the Bible, though read selectively so as to ignore belief in the presence of Jesus Christ in the Eucharist, the sacred character of marriage and the importance of works for salvation. Thus, there is a threatening crisis for Christianity that could constitute a second Reformation through the proscription of beliefs and a renewal of persecution, but one more insidious than the first Reformation because it is partially intra-mural, its leaders gaining spurious power from their tendency to ally themselves with established secular society's moral and philosophical relativism. Lethargy in the Church is a residue of the Reformation, with the Catholic population of England still subject to the influence of the established Church and mesmerised by secular society, and thus hampered in making a creative or courageous response. As was true for Philip, there is little solace coming from public advocates of the faith since the fear of falling foul of secular powers discourages many Christian leaders and thinkers. Believers must be ready for sacrifice and judgement, and their only hope is similar to that held by Philip: undying faith in God's love, mercy and justice. We can surely hope for the help of St Philip's prayers for restoration of the true faith and reconciliation between Catholics and Protestants.

Concerning St Philip's prayer life and thus the power of his intercession, we have seen that he was a man without compromise in his faith and his spiritual priorities, in his devotion to the Blessed Virgin through the Rosary, and in his remorse for the sins and failings of his early life, especially his treatment of his wife. There is the zeal he showed for the things of God by his rule of life, his confronting the realities of death and eternity by his readiness for his execution, the importance he attached to the Mass and sacraments by having a priest in residence in his London home, and his gratitude to those bringing him their spiritual help, including especially Fr Weston, who reconciled him to the Catholic faith, and Fr Southwell, who brought him comfort through his letters. Above all, Philip trusted in God for the final outcome and was content to offer the sacrifice of his life for the Church and for the love of God, as we saw from the testament letter that he penned in readiness for his expected execution.

So, was Philip's a wasted life, as presumably the Queen and her courtiers imagined? Most definitely not! The message of the saints is their faith in the supreme Good, but it is valuable to trace this out in the life of one who was not just a saint but a man who accepted death for his beliefs and who is thus a martyr-witness to the truth. This is the example that St Philip offers, a heart generous in repentance and love, one that is surely united in prayer with faithful Christians of every age who are called to detach themselves from the world in fidelity to the truth.

✢ 8 ✢

Reclaiming the Elizabethan Martyrs

W E CAN LOOK TO THE SAINTS AND MARTYRS for the
answer as to how we are to live as Christians. St
Teresa of Calcutta and Pope St John Paul II typify
people who operated oblivious to the polemical character of
the issues that arose around them. They ploughed their lives'
furrows, trusting in God. And there are many in all walks of
life who do the same, often hidden from view. These are the
clergy, religious, parents, medical personnel, and so forth,
who really do make the world go round, or go round God's
way. If we speak of reclaiming the martyrs, this is no historical
project. By remembering and honouring the martyrs, we give
God glory for the holiness with which he has invested them.
The Elizabethan martyrs are a corroboration of St Irenaeus'
famous words, 'The glory of God is man fully alive, and the
life of man is the vision of God'. In their human variety, their
different vocations in life, their pains and endurance, and even
in the joy with which they went to the block or the gallows,
they are the glorious company of martyrs in the Communion
of Saints in whom we can place our trust.[1]

Despite the rejection by Protestants of the significance of
the role in glory of the saints and martyrs, they remain of
vital importance for Catholics, and perhaps in a special way
in England. They are perennial witnesses to the country, both

---

[1]   See Appendix B for a listing of the names of the Forty Martyrs of
England and Wales and the dates of their feast-days. In addition to
these forty saints, there were fifty martyrs beatified by Pope Leo XIII,
one hundred and seven beatified by Pope Pius XI, and eighty-five
beatified by Pope John Paul II.

Church and State. They, and particularly the martyrs, inspire us by their commitment to faith. The Church comes to new life through their deaths. Their prayer is certainly for the liberty and exaltation of the Church and the restoration of the old faith. Without their fortitude and faith, we could falter, wondering if it was all make-believe. The saints are more than willing to intercede on our behalf, but their prayers are less availing if the faithful are not seriously asking for their intercession. The Body of Christ needs our prayers. It is a collective effort of the whole Church. Moreover, our own sacrifices and hardships are a part of this treasury of grace, a necessary participation of the faithful in the very cause for which they are seeking the prayers of the martyrs. The saints have shown us the direction in which to find the truth. We would be ignoring and squandering their sacrifice if we failed to follow them.

It is difficult to imagine that Philip could ever have abandoned the course he had chosen and revert to being a loyal member of the Elizabethan establishment. It is as if the existence of the evil and injustice that he experienced cast him into the arms of truth and goodness. Similarly, today, we look at the secular world and see that it offers us almost nothing in which we can put our faith, and so we turn to the truth of the Word of God, the goodness of the Cross and the beauty of the Catholic faith and liturgy. In this we follow the martyrs. They have entered by the narrow gate and are waiting for us to join them. Because of their gratitude for the love and mercy shown to them by the Lord they see themselves as like the prodigal son, who 'was dead and came back to life, was lost and is found' (Lk 15: 32), and it is certain that by their prayers they will help their countrymen to revive, and to overcome the evils of a later time.

THE COMMUNION OF THE MARTYR-SAINTS

The extraordinary thing is that even the martyrs depended upon the saints who had preceded them. Philip might not have had his conversion had it not been for St Edmund Campion, and St Edmund explicitly affirmed he was following in the footsteps of the very saints and confessors of England that those trying him were rejecting. Similarly, St Robert Southwell must have been inspired by St Edmund Campion, and he, in turn, was able to encourage and inspire St Philip Howard through his letters; and perhaps the example of Philip's constancy in the Tower was a help to St Robert in ensuring his faithfulness to the Lord to death. These three, Edmund, Robert and Philip, are brother-martyrs in more than one sense, since not only were they fellow-sufferers in the Elizabethan persecution but their lives were linked by circumstance, so that there was an interplay of inspiration and grace as they progressed towards their common destiny.

It is worth pondering the actual words used by these men in their final messages or speeches to see how closely in communion they were. In their readiness for martyrdom they declared:

> To be condemned with these old lights, not of England only, but of the world, by their degenerate descendants, is both gladness and glory to us. (St Edmund)[2]

> I deliver my soul into the hands of God my Creator, earnestly beseeching Him that He may preserve and strengthen it with His grace and grant it to continue faithful in this final conflict. (St Robert)[3]

> And I do most firmly, resolutely and unmoveably hold and believe this One, Holy, Catholic, and Apostolic Faith. And as I will die in the same so am I most ready at all times, if need be, to yield my life for defence thereof. (St Philip) (AM, pp. 99–102).

In their adherence to the Catholic faith they were at one:

> In condemning us you condemn all your own ancestors, all the ancient priests, Bishops and Kings: all that was once the glory of England, the Island of Saints, and the most devoted child of the See of Peter. For what have we taught ... that they did not uniformly teach? (St Edmund)

---

[2] From the speech cited in https://catholicinsight.com/the-diamond-of-england-the-mission-and-martyrdom-of-st-edmund-campion.
[3] Cited in the Preface of Southwell, *The Complete Works*, pp. xxi–xxiii.

For I die because I am a Catholic priest, elected into
the Society of Jesus in my youth; nor has any other
thing, during the last three years in which I have been
imprisoned, been charged against me. (St Robert)

For albeit I must acknowledge myself most frail, and a
heinous sinner, yet as I am bound to maintain in myself
the name and faith of a Catholic man (which next unto
God I hold in greatest price and account, and which
every faithful Christian ought to esteem above all other
things whatsoever). (St Philip)

They go to their deaths unanimously denying being guilty
of treason:

As to the treasons which have been laid to my charge,
and for which I am come here to suffer, I desire you all
to bear witness with me that I am thereof altogether
innocent. I am a Catholic man and a priest; in that
Faith have I lived and in that Faith I intend to die. If
you esteem my religion treason, then am I guilty; as for
other treason I never committed any, God is my judge.
(St Edmund)

Then as regards the Queen (to whom I have never done
nor wished any evil), I have daily prayed for her. (St
Robert)

I here protest before His Divine Majesty and all the Holy
Court of Heaven, that I have committed no treason,
and that the Catholic and Roman Faith which I hold,
is the only cause (as far as I can any way imagine) why
either I have been thus long imprisoned, or for which
I am now ready to be executed. (St Philip)

And all three conclude their final messages with a prayer for
the Queen:

Wherein have I offended her? In this I am innocent.
This is my last speech; in this give me credit . . . I have
and do pray for her. Yea, for Elizabeth your Queen and
my Queen, unto whom I wish a long quiet reign with
all prosperity. (St Edmund)

[I] . . . now with all my heart do pray, that from His
great mercy, through the wounds and most worthy

merits of Christ His son, He may grant that she may use the ample gifts and endowments wherewith He has endowed her, to the immortal glory of His name, the prosperity of the whole nation, and the eternal welfare of her soul and body. (St Robert)

And thus I will conclude with beseeching Almighty God the Father of mercies, and God of all consolation to grant peace unto His Church, charity and grace to mine enemies, salvation and felicity to the Queen, and realm. (St Philip)

St Philip is an example of hope and trust in God for all those Christians, such as the poor, the sick, the old, the lonely, the disabled, and indeed all who have faith, hope and love in their hearts, who see the moral and spiritual needs of today's world and who, while prevented by their incapacity from intervening practically, can devote themselves to prayer. He is already seen as an inspiration for our time by being taken as a patron of the diocese of Arundel and Brighton in England and of many schools. He would surely welcome us as pilgrims to his shrine in Arundel Cathedral and to the Tyburn Convent Martyrs' Chapel, in London, near the site of the infamous Tyburn Tree, the scaffold on which so many martyrs were hanged, to pray for the restoration of the true faith to England in 'a Catholick time', as Philip put it in a letter to his wife (AM, p. 159).

If we forget such a martyr, we would be counting his life as lived in vain or as an irrelevance, when every hardship he suffered can be an encouragement to us to believe, to trust and to obey God's will. St Philip saw the Truth that would make him free. Insofar as we face the truth in our lives, we accept the part offered to us by the Lord as our sharing in his sufferings. We cannot look upon St Philip's martyrdom from afar and say it does not concern us. As with the Passion of Jesus, evoked in St Paul's words, 'in my flesh I am completing what is lacking in Christ's afflictions for the sake of his body, that is, the Church' (Col 1: 24), we too have to make up what is lacking by our own endorsement of or participation in the experience of the martyrs. Otherwise, how can we expect God's mercy on a world filled with so much collective and unrepented guilt?

The Noble Martyr

'THE BLOOD OF THE MARTYRS IS THE SEED OF THE CHURCH' (TERTULLIAN)

The martyrs of the Penal Times are at risk of being forgotten or relegated to the status of images or figures stuck in history. This is all the more unjust when we reflect that they are a flowering of a much greater number of Catholic recusants who shared their spirit. In a remarkable piece of personal research conducted over a period of thirty years, Malcolm Pullan has compiled a history of the Penal Times with portraits of a large number of these heroic but largely forgotten figures, people whom he suggests could justifiably have been declared martyrs had their names been put forward by the Catholic Church in England.[4] Pullan instances Francis Tregian, a landed gentleman who was totally dispossessed of his property on account of his Catholic faith, and spent a total of twenty-seven years in prison before finally being exiled. He died in Portugal in 1608, and seventeen years later his body was found to be incorrupt. Another example cited is Fr William Weston SJ, the renowned and holy priest who reconciled St Philip to the Church, who spent seventeen years in prison simply because of his priesthood and then was exiled and died in Spain.

These are just two of the hundreds of Catholics who took a stand against the authorities, against the received wisdom of their day, against the powers that had the strength to confine, punish and even execute them, but who had the spirit to gainsay them and to hold onto the truth vouchsafed to them by God. They are waiting to be given their deserved role in the spiritual revival of English and indeed western Catholicism and society. They died for this cause and so must care for it no less than do the faithful among our contemporaries. Must they wait until the state of these societies reaches an extreme of unbelief, spiritual darkness and persecution of Christian faith for us to turn to them for their prayers?

While this work has been written to highlight the life of one martyr as a step in encouraging the reclaiming of all such holy

---

[4]   M. Pullan, *The Lives and Times of the Forty Martyrs of England and Wales 1535–1680* (London: New Generation Publishing, 2013).

men and women in England, it is evident that a similar appeal could be made in many other countries where the Church is threatened and is in need of spiritual revival. There is a history of persecution in Ireland, France, Mexico, Poland, Ukraine, China and Iraq, to cite only some of the most striking cases, where there have been untold numbers kept in captivity till their deaths, tortured or deliberately killed for their faith. In all these societies, the martyrs' countrymen have a sacred responsibility to remember them and to seek their prayers for the flourishing of the Church in their own times.

St Philip, who was once forsaken in his prison cell, can especially be a help to those who feel in their weakness and isolation that their lives lack significance. It is when their faith feels weak that Catholic Christians need to look to the saints and martyrs and pray for their intercession, calling on their witness and spiritual strengths, asking them for their wisdom and counsel, trusting in them confidently. As has been said, 'They buried us, but they did not know we were seeds'. If we remember their struggles and adversities, seek to identify with their faith and hope and to imitate their virtues, praying to them as friends and brethren, we can help to make the martyrs better known and revered. By such means we will be giving them their rightful role as intercessors and guides in contributing to the restoration of truth, goodness and the beauty of holiness to the Church and we can be confident of a divine blessing with the help of the prayers of Mary, Queen of Martyrs. As a sign of hope, the initiative of the Bishops of England and Wales in re-dedicating England as the Dowry of Mary on the Solemnity of the Annunciation in 2020, 'in the wrackes of Walsingham', is perhaps a harbinger of a renewal of interest in the legacy of the Elizabethan Martyrs. There can be no doubt that this cause is precious to the martyrs and that Heaven is waiting for a re-awakening of the faithful to their witness and to the power of their intercession in order to show its generosity in graces for Mary's Dowry.

APPENDIX A

Fuller Versions
of Some Writings Cited

A LETTER FROM PHILIP HOWARD
TO FR ROBERT SOUTHWELL

IN WHICH HE SETS OUT THE CASE
FOR HIS INNOCENCE OF THE CRIME OF TREASON

Seeing Almighty God hath vouchsafed of his infinit goodness to call me being the meanest of all his servants, and most unworthy, I must confess, of so great honour to bear witness of the Catholick Faith, and Roman Church, I thought it fit, for preventing of all sinister practices, which might be used either to the disgrace of my faith or discredit of my self, to testify that under my hand, in as effectual manner as I could, which I am ready to seal with my blood, by the grace and assistance of our Lord, whensoever need and occasion shall require: that neither the innocency of my mind, nor integrity of mine actions may be defaced by the untrue suggestions of others (as to men in my state it often happens) nor my firm resolution in the Catholick and Roman Faith, perverted by the false reports of evill disposed persons.

For albeit I must acknowledge my self most frail, and a heinous sinner, yet as I am bound to maintain in my self the name and faith of a Catholick man (which next unto God I hold in greatest price and account, and which every faithfull Christian ought to esteem above all other things whatsoever) so do I most desire that all men should take me for such an one, as in truth I am ; and that no man should be either mislead or beguiled

by malicious and untrue reports to think otherwise of
me, then both my words and deeds do plainly testifie.

Wherefore for the satisfaction of all men. and discharge
of my conscience before God, I here protest before His
Divine Majesty and all the Holy Court of Heaven, that
I have committed no treason, and that the Catholick
and Roman Faith which I hold, is the only cause (as
far as I can any way imagine) why either I have been
thus long imprisoned, or for which I am now ready
to be executed. And I do most firmly, resolutely and
unmoveably hold and believe this One, Holy, Catholick,
and Apostolick Faith. And as I will die in the same so
am I most ready at all times, if need be, to yield my life
for defence thereof.

And whatsoever the most sacred Council of Trent hath
established touching faith and manners, I believe and
hold. And whatsoever it hath condemned, I condemn in
my soul, and renounce here under my hand, and abjure
from the bottom of my heart. And I do most earnestly
desire, that all Catholicks conceive this opinion of me,
and take me so, as I have protested myself to be, and
not credit any untrue reports that have, may, or shall
be spread of me to the contrary: for as Christ is life
unto me, so account I death a most happy and glorious
gain unto me being in defence of His Faith, and for His
Holy Name.

And thus I will conclude with beseeching Almighty
God the Father of mercies, and God of all consolation
to grant peace unto His Church, charity and grace to
mine enemies, salvation and felicity to the Queen, and
realm, and to me as an untimely fruit (being born before
my time) and the meanest of all His servants a constant
perseverance in His Holy Faith and love of His Divine
Majesty. Amen.

By me a most humble and obedient child of
the Catholick Roman Church. Philipp Howard.

(AM, pp. 99–102)

94

POEMS BY ST PHILIP HOWARD

FOURE-FOULD MEDITATION, OF THE FOURE LAST THINGS

Verses from the four parts of the poem, with its original spelling[1]

Of the Houre of Death

O wretched man, which lovest earthie thinges,
And to this worlde hast made thyselfe a thrall,
Whose shorte delightes eternall sorrow bringes,
Whose sweete in shewe in trewth is bitter gall:
Whose pleasures fade eare scarse they be possest,
And greve him lest that most doe them detest. (v.1)

The tyme will come when death will thee assalte:
Conceive it then as present for to bee,
That thou in tyme maiest seeke to mend thie falte,
And in thie life thine errors plainlye see:
Imagen now thie corse is almost spent,
And marke thie frinds how deepelie they lament. (v.3)

What doste thou thinke, now all thie sences faile?
What doste thou saye by pleasure here is wonne?
How dost thou now thie passed life bewayle?
dost thou wishe thie course were new to ronne?
What woldst thou doe thie endinge life to save?
What woldst thou geve for that thou canst not have? (v.7)

Thou waylest now the pleasinge of thie will,
Thie evill gott goods doth make thee so lament,
Thie vaine delightes with anguishe thee doth fill,
Thie wantone tricks thie conscience doth torment:
Thie sweetest sinnes doth bringe thee bitter smarte,
Thie heynous faultes oppresse thie dyinge harte. (v.10)

Thye flesh shall serve for maggots for a praye,
For pampering which both sea and land was sought,
Thie bodie must tranceformed be to claye,
For whose delight suche costlie clothes were bought:
Thie pryde in dust, thie glorie in the grave,
Thie flesh in earth their endinge now shall have. (v.17)

[1] Selected from the 119 verses of the 1606 edition, reprinted 1895.

The Noble Martyr

Of the Day of Judgement

Thou syted arte a just account to showe,
How farre thou sought thie selfe for to deny,
How all thie landes and welth thou didst bestowe,
And with thie goodes thie brothers wante supplye:
What care thou hadst thie makers name to prayse,
What paine thou tokst to walk in all his ways. (v. 25)

If eke thie foes revenge thou haste not wrought,
If to thie frindes thou never wert unkinde,
If earthlie pompe thou ever sett att nought,
If secrett hate thou haste not kept in mynde:
If thou alike didst joye and sorrowe take,
And with thie harte all carnall lust forsake. (v. 27)

Thye thoughtes and words the Judge dothe open laye,
And asketh now a strayte account of all,
How thou didst here his motions obaye,
And for his grace with erenest fervor call:
If all thie life on earth thou ledst upright,
And in his love didst sett thie whole delight. (v. 28)

Then comes the Devill, and to our Lord doth saye,
'O righteous Judge, this wretche I ought to have,
For in his lyfe he would not thee obaye,
But with his harte to mee him selfe he gave:
My precepts eke he practist daye and night,
And mee to please he made his whole delight.' (v. 34)

O wretched man! How heavie is thie harte,
How dost thou wish for that which can not bee,
How dost though sigh and quake in everie parte,
And must thie frinds be severd thus from thee:
They fild with joye in glorie now shall raigne,
And full of greife thou torment must sustaine. (v. 54)

Of the Paines of Hell

If for a while noe creature can endure
In earthly fiere one member for to bee,
What torments doe thy passed joys procure,
In endlesse flames thy members all to see!

What greefe, what paine, what sorrowes doe they breed,
Which earthly flames in all doe farre exceede! (v. 63)

Thy torments strange doe breede thee bitter greefe,
And reste in thine imagination still,
Thyne owne conceipte which now should yeld releese,
Doth labour more with sorrow thee to fill:
Thou thinkest most what most thou wouldst eschew,
Thy griefe thy thoughts, and thoughts thy griefe
*   renew.* (v. 65)

Thy memory doth call unto thy mynde
The shorte delight of all thy pleasures past.
It wounds thy harte these paines for them to finde,
Which greveous are and shall for ever last:
Thy desperate case no comfort can obtaine
Thy passed joys increase thy present paine. (v. 66)

If I my sinnes with sorrowe had confest,
They had to me bene clene remitted all:
In stead of greefe, I glorie had possest,
If I for grace had bent my minde to call:
O wretched wretch, that for so small a paine,
Refusinge blisse, in torment must remaine. (v. 70)

O dampned soule! Howe dost thou roare and crye!
What deadlie greefes thee daylie doe oppresse!
But lyft a whyle thie cursed eies on hye,
And see what joys the blessed their possesse:
That by the sight, thie torments maye increase,
And for thie losse thie sorrowes never cease. (v. 86)

Of the Joyes of Heaven

Those sacred Saintes remaine in perfect peace.
Which Christ confessed, and walked in his wayes,
They swim in blisse, which now shall never ceace.
And singinge all, his name do ever prayse:
Before His throne in white they daylie stand,
And carrie palmes of triumph in their handes. (v. 94)

Above them all the Virgin hath a place.
Which cawsd the world with comfort to abound;

The Noble Martyr

The beames doe shine in her unspotted face,
And with the starres her head is richlye crownd;
In glory shee all creatures passeth farr,
The moone her shooes, the sunn her garments are. (v. 96)

And next to her, but in a higher throne.
Our Saviour in his manhode sitteth here;
From whom proceedes all perfect joye alone.
And in whose face all glorie doth appere:
The Saintes' delight conceyved cannot be
When they a man the Lord of anngells see. (v. 99)

To thinke on this it passeth humaine witt:
The more we thinke the lesse we come to knowe;
He dothe upon his Fathers right hand sitt,
And all the Saintes their humble service showe:
His sight to them doth endlesse comfort bringe,
And they to him all prayses ever singe. (v. 102)

They here possesse what maye content them most,
And nothinge wante that perfect blisse maye bringe:
With all delight here breathes the Holye Ghost.
Which alwayes makes a freshe and endlesse springe:
Noe daye is here, noe morninge, noone, nor night,
But ever one and alwayes shininge bright. (v. 114)

A MEDITATION ON CHRIST'S PASSION[2]

O Christe my Lorde which for my sinnes didst hang upon a tree,
Graunt that thie grace in mee poore wretch may still engrafted be.

Graunt that thy naked hanging there may kill in me all pride,
And care of wealth, sith thow didst then in such poore state abide.

Graunt that thie crown of pricking thornes which thou for me
*   didst weare,*
May make me willing for thy sake all shame and payne to beare.

Graunt that those skornes and tauntes which thow didst on the
*   crosse endure,*
May humble me and in my harte all pacience still procure.

Graunt that thy praying for thy foes may plant within my brest,
Such charitie as from my harte I malice may detest.

Graunt that thy pierced handes which did of nothing all thinges
*   frame,*
May move mee to lift up my handes and ever prayse thy name.

Graunt that thy wounded feete whose steppes were perfect
*   evermore,*
May learne my feete to treade those pathes which thow hast gon
*   before.*

Graunt that thy bitter gall which did thy emptie body fill,
May teache mee to subdue my self and to performe thy holy will.

Graunt that thy woundes may cure the sores which sinne in me
*   hath wrought,*
Graunt that thy death my save the soule which with thy blood was
*   bought.*

Graunt that those droppes of blood which ran out from thy harte
*   amayne,*
May meeke my harte into salt teares to see thy grievous payne.

Graunt that thy blessed grave whereas thy bodie lay awhile,
May burie all such vaine delights as may my mynd defile.

---

[2]   Reprinted in Guiney, *Recusant Poets*, pp. 227–8.

The Noble Martyr

Graunt that thy going downe to them that did thy sighte desire,
May keep my sowle when I am dead cleane from the purging fire.

Graunt that thy rising up from death, may rayse my thoughts
* from sinne,*
Graunt that thy parting from this earth, from earth my harte may
* winne.*

Graunt Lorde that thy ascending then may lifte my mynd to thee,
That there my harte and joye may reste, though here in flesh I be.

Poems by St Philip Howard

A LAMENT
FOR OUR LADY'S SHRINE AT WALSINGHAM[3]

In the wracks of Walsingham
Whom should I choose
But the Queen of Walsingham
to be my guide and muse.

Then, thou Prince of Walsingham,
Grant me to frame
Bitter plaints to rue thy wrong,
Bitter woe for thy name.

Bitter was it so to see
The seely sheep
Murdered by the ravenous wolves
While the shepherds did sleep.

Bitter was it, O to view
The sacred vine,
Whilst the gardeners played all close,
Rooted up by the swine.

Bitter, bitter, O to behold
The grass to grow
Where the walls of Walsingham
So stately did show.

Such were the worth of Walsingham
While she did stand,
Such are the wracks as now do show
Of that Holy Land.

Level, level, with the ground
The towers do lie,
Which, with their golden glittering tops,
Pierced once to the sky.

Where were gates are no gates now,
The ways unknown

---

[3] This version, with modernised spelling, is that re-printed in J. Saward et al. (eds), *Firmly I Believe and Truly: The Spiritual Tradition of Catholic England* (Oxford: Oxford University Press, 2011), pp. 167–8.

The Noble Martyr

Where the press of peers did pass
While her fame was blown.

Owls do scrike where the sweetest hymns
Lately were sung,
Toads and serpents hold their dens
Where the palmers did throng.

Weep, weep, O Walsingham,
Whose days are nights,
Blessings turned to blasphemies,
Holy deeds to despites.

Sin is where Our Lady sat,
Heaven is turned to hell,
Satan sits where Our Lord did sway –
Walsingham, O farewell!

A HYMN WHEREIN THE PRAISES OF ALL CREATURES
ARE OFFERED UP UNTO THE CREATOR[4]

O Christ, the glorious Crown
Of virgins that are pure,
Who dost a love and thirst for Thee
With – in their minds procure;
Thou art the Spouse of those
That chaste and humble be,
The hope, the life, the only help
Of such as trust in Thee.

All charity of those
Whose souls Thy love doth warm;
All simple plainness of such minds
As think no kind of harm;
All sweet delights wherewith
The patient hearts abound,
Do blaze Thy Name, and with Thy praise
They make the world resound.

The sky, the land, the sea.
And all on earth below.
The glory of Thy worthy Name,
Do with their praises show.
The winter yields Thee praise.
And summer doth the same;
The sun, the moon, the stars and all,
Do magnify Thy Name.

The roses that appear
So fair in outward sight;
The violets which with their scent
Do yield so great delight;
The pearls, the precious stones,
The birds, Thy praise do sing;
The woods, the wells, and all delights
Which from this earth do spring.

---

[4]   The version re-printed in the Arundel Hymnal, with the added note:
'written in the Tower of London by Philip Howard, Earl of Arundel'.

The Noble Martyr

What creature, O sweet Lord,
From praising Thee can stay?
What earthly thing, but filled with joy.
Thine honour doth bewray?
Let us therefore with praise.

Thy mighty works express,
With heart and hand, with mind and all
Which we from Thee possess.

A POEM BY ROBERT SOUTHWELL

I DYE WITHOUT DESERT[5]

If orphane childe, enwrapt in swathing bands,
Doth move to mercy when forlorne it liyes,
If none without remorse of love withstands
The pitiouse noyse of infante's selye cryes:
Then hope, my helplesse hart, some tender eares
Will rue thy orphane state and feeble teares.

Relinquished lamb, in solitarye wood.
With dying bleat doth move the toughest mynde;
The gasping pangues of new engendered brood
Base though they be, compassion use to find:
Why should I then of pitty doubt to speede,
Whose bapp would force the hardest hart to bleede ?

Left orphan like in helples state I rue,
With only sighes and teares I plead my case:
My dying plaintes I daylie do renewe.
And fill with heavy noise a desert place.
Some tender heart will weep to hear me mone,
Men pity may, but help me, God alone.

Rayne down yee heavens! your teares this case requires.
Man's eyes unable are enough to shedd.
If sorrowes could have place in heavenly choirs,
A juster ground the world hath seldom bredd.
For right is wrong'd, and virtue wag'd with blood ;
The bad are bliss'd, God murdred in the good.

A gracious plant for fruite, for leafe, for flower,
A peerless gem for virtue, proof and price,
A noble peer for prowess, wit and power,
A friend to truth, a foe I was to vice.
And lo, alas! now innocent I die,
A case that might even make the stones to cry.

Thus Fortune's favoures still are bent to flighte.
Thus worldly blisse in fynall bale doth ende,

---

[5]   Southwell, *The Complete Works*, pp. 155–6.

The Noble Martyr

Thus virtue still pursued is with spighte.
But let my fate, though rueful, none offend.
God doth, sometimes, first cropp the sweetest flowre,
And leaves the weed, till Time doo it devoure.

APPENDIX B

Feast-days of the Forty Martyrs of England and Wales

21 January	St Alban Roe
1 February	St Henry Morse
21 February	St Robert Southwell
22 March	St Nicholas Owen
2 April	St John Payne
7 April	St Henry Walpole
4 May	Ss John Houghton, Robert Lawrence, Augustine Webster and Richard Reynolds (on this date all the Beatified Martyrs of England and Wales are commemorated)
30 May	St Luke Kirby
21 June	St John Rigby
23 June	St Thomas Garnet
28 June	St John Southworth
12 July	St John Jones
19 July	St John Plessington
22 July	Ss Philip Evans and John Lloyd
24 July	St John Boste
22 August	Ss John Wall & John Kemble
27 August	St David Lewis
28 August	St Edmund Arrowsmith
30 August	Ss Margaret Clitherow, Anne Line and Margaret Ward
10 September	St Ambrose Barlow
17 October	St Richard Gwyn
19 October	St Philip Howard

25 October	The Forty Martyrs of England and Wales
29 November	St Cuthbert Mayne
1 December	Ss Edmund Campion, Ralph Sherwin and Alexander Briant
5 December	St John Almond
10 December	Ss Swithun Wells, Edmund Gennings, Polydore Plasden, Eustace White and John Roberts
23 December	St John Stone

BIBLIOGRAPHY

MAIN SOURCES

Fitzalan-Howard, H. G., Duke of Norfolk (ed.), *The Lives of Philip Howard, Earl of Arundel, and of Anne Dacres, his Wife.* Charleston, SC: Nabu Press, 1857.

Pollen, J. H., and W. MacMahon, *Unpublished Documents Relating to the English Martyrs.* London: Catholic Record Society, 1908–19.

WRITINGS OF ST PHILIP HOWARD

Foure-fould Meditation, of the foure last things viz. 1 2 3 4 of the Houre of Death. Day of Judgement. Paines of Hell. Joys of Heaven. Shewing the estate of the Elect and Reprobate (published posthumously, 1606; reprinted London: Elkin Matthews, 1895).

Lanspergius, Johannes Justus, *An Epistle of Jesus Christ to the soule, that is devoutly affected towards him. Wherein are contained certaine divine inspirations, teaching a man to know himself, & instructing him in the perfection of true piety.* (Philip Howard's translation, posthumously published, 1610).

Letter to the Queen, 11–15 April 1585, in Fitzalan-Howard, *The Lives of Philip Howard.*

OTHER WORKS CITED OR CONSULTED

Allen, W., *A True, Sincere and Modest Defence of English Catholics that Suffer for their Faith both at home and abroad, against a False, Seditious and Slanderous Libel, entitled 'The Execution of Justice in England'.* Rheims, 1584.

Arundel Cathedral, *Saint Philip Howard, Earl of Arundel.* Stroud: Pitkin Publishing, 2015.

Benedict XVI, *Values in a Time of Upheaval* (San Francisco: Ignatius Press, 2006).

Brennan, M. *Martyrs of the English Reformation.* Kansas: Angelus Press, 1991.

Campion, E., *To the Right Honourable, the Lords of Her Majesty's Privy Council* (Campion's Brag), 1580.

—— *Decem Rationes, To the Learned Members of the Universities of Oxford and Cambridge*, 1581.

Caraman, P., *Henry Garnet 1555–1605 and the Gunpowder Plot*. London: Longman, Green & Co., 1964.

—— *Henry Morse: Priest of the Plague and Martyr of England*. London: Fontana Books, 1952.

Dreher, R., *The Benedict Option: A Strategy for Christians in a Post-Christian Nation*. New York: Sentinel, 2017.

Catholic Encyclopedia (http://www.newadvent.org).

Cumming, J. (ed.), *Letters from Saints to Sinners*. London: Burns & Oates, 1996.

Duffy, E., *The Stripping of the Altars: Traditional Religion in England c. 1400–c. 1580*. Newhaven: Yale University Press, 1992.

Farmer, D. H., *The Oxford Dictionary of Saints*. Oxford: Oxford University Press, 1992.

Gerard, J., *The Autobiography of a Hunted Priest*. San Francisco: Ignatius Press, 2012.

Goodman, G., *The Court of King James the First*. Boston: Adamant Media Corp., 2002.

Granada, L. de, *La Guía de Pecadores*. Lisbon, 1556. Recently published in translation as *The Sinners' Guide*. Charlotte: Tan Books, 2014.

Guiney, L. I., *Recusant Poets*. London: Sheed & Ward, 1939.

Hogge, A., *God's Secret Agents*. London: Harper Perennial, 2006.

More, H., *Historia Provinciae Anglicanae*, 1660.

Newdigate, C. A., 'A new chapter in the life of Bl. Robert Southwell SJ', *The Month* 157 (1931) pp. 246–54.

Newman, St John Henry, *Second Spring* (sermon), http://www.newmanreader.org.

Pullan, M., *The Lives and Times of the Forty Martyrs of England and Wales 1535–1680*. London: New Generation Publishing, 2013.

Relazione del promotore generale della fede, intorno ai martiri d'Inghilterra, 27 October 1929 (Jesuits in Britain Archives).

Robinson, J. M., *The Dukes of Norfolk*. Chichester: Phillimore, 1995.

Saward, J., *et al.* (eds), *Firmly I Believe and Truly: The Spiritual Tradition of Catholic England*. Oxford: Oxford University Press, 2011.

Southwell, R., 'The Triumphs over Death', in *Southwell's Works*, ed. W. J. Walter. London: Keating & Co., 1822.

—— 'An Epistle of Comfort to reverend priests and to the honourable, worshipful and others of the lay sort restrained in durance for the Catholic faith', in *Southwell's Works*, ed. W. J. Walter. London: Keating & Co., 1822.

—— *The Complete Works with Life and Death*. London: D. Stewart, 1876.

Waugh, E., *Edmund Campion, Jesuit and Martyr*. London: Penguin, 2012.

Lightning Source UK Ltd.
Milton Keynes UK
UKHW011238091119
353155UK00001B/3/P